POLICING EOKA :

The United Kingdom Police Unit to Cyprus

1955 - 1960

A duplicated magazine for the EOKA youth movement
Αακιμου Νεολαιασ Εοκα, urging them to 'do their duty'.

POLICING EOKA :

The United Kingdom Police Unit to Cyprus

1955 - 1960

Richard Cowley

Peg and Whistle Books
(an Imprint of Monkshood Publishing)
Barton Seagrave
Kettering
Northamptonshire
2008

ISBN 0 9534095 1 1

Published by Peg and Whistle Books
An Imprint of

Monkshood Publishing
20 Grosvenor Way
Barton Seagrave
Kettering
Northamptonshire NN15 6TG

Printed and Bound in Great Britain by
BookPrintingUK.com
Remus House
Coltsfoot Drive
Woodston
Peterborough
Cambridgeshire PE2 9JX

Set in
Times New Roman

CONTENTS

R ichard Cowley is a retired Northamptonshire Police officer. Born in Finedon in Northamptonshire, he became an apprentice compositor in the printing trade. Subsequently, he worked in estimating and production planning before becoming a typographer and graphic designer. He still retains a keen interest in printing history and typography.

In 1968 he joined the then Northampton and County Constabulary as a Special Constable before joining the regular constabulary two years later. Always stationed in the north of the county, he served in large towns, small villages, desk jobs and specialist squads, and along the way, picked up his interest in police, criminal and legal history.

He graduated from the Open University with a BA in Modern History, before going on to gain an MA in Victorian Studies from Leicester University. He has written four previous books : *Policing Northamptonshire 1836-1986* (1986); *Guilty M'Lud! The criminal history of Northamptonshire* (1998); *Who's Buried Where in Northamptonshire* (2000); and *A History of Northamptonshire Police* (being published November 2008). In 2005 he was commissioned by the Home Office to write the history of the Inspectorate of Constabulary for the 150th anniversary of its establishment.

Now retired, he is the Curator and Archivist of Northamptonshire Police; and also the Curator and Archivist of Northamptonshire Saint John Ambulance, of which he has been a member for 25 years, and which in 2006 awarded him the dignity of a Serving Brother of the Venerable Order of Saint John of Jerusalem.

Married to Valerie, they both enjoy their six grand-children and two great-grand-children; and holiday in Cyprus whenever they can.

INTRODUCTION

Although the history of the Cyprus problems of 1955 to 1960 is well known, together with the armed forces' role in it, what is not so well known is that a contingent of British police officers – both men and women - also went to the island, and made a great contribution. Having served myself with two former members of this contingent (The United Kingdom Police Unit - the UKU) during my own police career, I was already aware of the Unit's existence. So after visiting Cyprus myself, I looked for a written history of it.

Sadly, but not surprisingly, I found this had never attracted a historian. British police history is very much an under researched field, and the number of police history books remains remarkably low. The British police service is one of the essential ingredients of a civilised society, and is in evidence every single day of the year, right in front of our very eyes, yet the knowledge of police history is ashamedly low, or even non-existent.

This book is my own small contribution in trying to rectify this indifference, and is the result of more than ten years research. I hope it is an acceptable memorial to the officers of the UKU who lost their lives, and I further hope that it pays tribute to those members of it who are still with us. To them, this book is dedicated, in gratitude, and in appreciation of the enormous help I received from the UKU Old Comrades' Association.

This, at last, is their story.

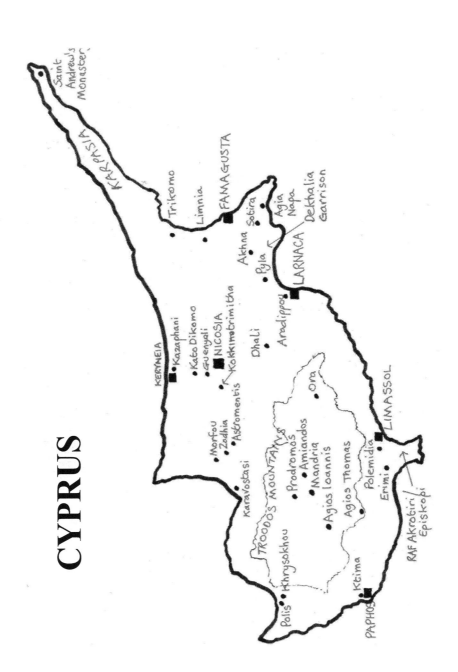

CYPRUS

Saint Andrew's Monaster.

KARPASIA

Trikomo

Limnia

FAMAGUSTA

Sotira

Agia Napa

Dekhalia Garrison

Akhna

Pyla

LARNACA

Aradippou

KERYNEIA

Kazaphani

Kato Dikomo

Guenyeli

NICOSIA

Kokkimotrimitha

DhaLi

Astromentis

Morfou

Zodhia

Astromentis

ora

Karavostasi

TROODOS MOUNTAINS

Prodromos

Amiandos

Mnandria

Agios Ioannis

Agios Thomas

Polemidia

Erimi

LIMASSOL

Palis Khrysokhou

Ktima

PAPHOS

RAF Akrotiri / Episkobi

THE BACKGROUND

Too small to exist by itself and too large to ignore, Cyprus has been squabbled over by the major powers for hundreds of years. Its strategic position on the main routes between Europe and Asia has ensured a succession of conquering, occupying powers since time began.

However, one element remained constant throughout - the survival of the Greek language and culture, even after the Turkish conquest of 1571. And although they lived fairly peaceably side by side with the Turkish Cypriots for 350 years or so, it was always the wish of the Greek Cypriots to form a union with their motherland, Greece.

Formed in the early nineteenth century, the movement for union with Greece, 'Enosis' (from the Greek Ενοσις, to make one, to unite) gradually gained momentum, much to the natural concern of the Turkish Cypriots. It was onto this stage that the British stepped in 1878 when the Cyprus Convention gave them control over the island.

Things were never easy for the British. Enosis, and the constant agitation for it, continued to be a major part of the island's politics. Major demonstrations occurred in 1880, 1897 and 1906, sometimes with loss of life.

Attempting to calm things down, in 1907, in his capacity as Parliamentary Under-Secretary for the Colonies, Winston Churchill visited Cyprus and met representatives of both Greek and Turkish communities. However, not even Churchill's famed diplomatic skills could overcome the depth of feeling, and he failed entirely to understand the situation. His fudging reply, saying that the views of the Turkish community on Cyprus must also be taken into account, alongside the Greek Cypriots' wishes for Enosis, satisfied neither faction, and Churchill left Cyprus with nothing resolved.

Thus, agitation for Enosis continued. And the Greek Cypriots' dreams were not helped either, by Britain's annexation of Cyprus in 1914, in retaliation against the Turkish alliance with Germany; and then by Cyprus being declared a British Crown Colony in 1925. The

Greek Cypriots realised that the British had no intentions of leaving the island, and thus Enosis was still as far away as it had ever been, and was not going to come easily.

But the desire for Enosis never diminished. And throughout these years, this desire was also fuelled by the so-called 'Great Idea', which was being formulated by the clergy and professional classes of mainland Greece - that of a Greater Hellas, uniting all Greeks under one flag, even those living under foreign governments. So the situation was becoming explosive.

And in 1931, the explosion came. In October of that year, anti-British riots had to be forcibly quelled with loss of life. The causes of these riots are complicated, but it was an acknowledged fact that the leadership of the Greek Orthodox Church on Cyprus was deeply involved in their organisation, as a means of throwing off colonial rule, and achieving Enosis. As a result, Bishops Nicodemus of Kition, and Makarios of Kyrenia were among ten Greek political leaders exiled from the island by the British.

The Archbishop of Cyprus at the time, Kyrillos III, was spared exile, as by then he was fairly elderly, and was allowed to continue in office, although with his powers very much reduced. When he died just two years later, the British put the archbishopric into 'abeyance', although the Greek Orthodox Church regarded Bishop Leontios of Paphos as the natural successor. Bishop Leontios had escaped exile in 1931, because fortuitously, at that very time, he had been a guest of the Archbishop of Canterbury in England. However, he was allowed to return to Cyprus only on the condition that he refrained from any political involvement. Thus, during the 1930s, agitation for Enosis went into a kind of lull, although the feeling was still simmering away underneath.

The Second World War also saw less open agitation for Enosis, as all sides combined against the common enemy of fascism. The contribution of Cyprus, however, was immense, the Cyprus Regiment being involved in all the European and African campaigns. And because of this military involvement, there was full employment on Cyprus itself. But following the peace in 1945, all that changed, and with the return of the soldiers, and no military work available, unemployment on the island became widespread, discontent started to seethe, industrial unrest broke out, and more riots had to be crushed. The subsequent trials and gaol sentences given to the union leaders resulted in the British being regarded as tyrants in suppressing legitimate trades unions.

And the desire for Enosis was now surfacing again. Although the archbishopric of Cyprus had been in abeyance since 1933, Bishop Leontios had been regarded as the natural successor. So when in October 1946, following the landslide victory of the Labour Party in Britain, the newly appointed Secretary for the Colonies, Arthur Creech Jones, in announcing a plan for a more liberal Constitution for Cyprus, also repealed the anti-ecclesiastical measures. Bishop Leontios was therefore confirmed as Archbishop of Cyprus, and was enthroned in June 1947. Archbishop Leontios, however, was chronically diabetic, and in less than one month he was dead. Replacing him, was Bishop Makarios of Kyrenia. But the new Archbishop Makarios II was that same Makarios who had been exiled in 1931 for his part in the anti-British pro-Enosis riots of that year. Not surprisingly, he immediately began calling for Enosis.

And also, just a few months later, in 1948, a certain Michael Mouskos, was consecrated Bishop of Kition, which is the diocese centred on Larnaca. And the new Bishop of Kition was also a fervent supporter of Enosis. So much so, that the Archbishop and Bishop organised a Church Plebiscite in January 1950. A massive 95.7% of the Greek Cypriot population voted for Enosis. However, just a few months later, Archbishop Makarios II died, and Michael Mouskos, Bishop of Kition, was elected to be the new archbishop, taking the title of Makarios III. In order to emphasise his intentions, Archbishop Makarios immediately started agitating for Enosis, and being more politically astute, took it a step further by placing it onto the international stage, by heading Cypriot delegations to Athens, London and New York.

At this point, obviously sensing more fervour in the Enosis campaign, a Greek Cypriot soldier, but failed politician, George Grivas, who had been a colonel in the Greek army, returned to Cyprus and met with Archbishop Makarios. Several meetings between the two men followed, both in Cyprus and in Athens. Grivas

3

was convinced that Enosis could only be achieved by violent, guerrilla tactics.

Makarios, however, maintained that only some form of sabotage and a policy of civil disobedience was all that was needed. After all, it had only been five years or so since Mahatma Gandhi had forced Indian independence from the British Empire, by using just those very methods. Gandhi's achievement must have been still fresh in the memory of Makarios, and he possibly thought that he could do the same in Cyprus, with himself as the spiritual and political leader. And this is probably why he resisted Grivas for two years.

However, Makarios was soon to have his mind made up for him. On 28 July 1954, Henry Hopkinson, the British Minister for Colonial Affairs, stated in the House of Commons that 'Cyprus was simply one of those territories that could never hope to be fully independent because of British defence obligations in the Middle East'. And so it was, that with just those two dozen words, words that still rankle with Cypriots today, Hopkinson unwittingly lit the fuse. By those words, he made bloodshed inevitable.

Makarios was thus finally convinced, that Britain was flatly refusing to consider Enosis. This was confirmed in the following December, when the United Nations also declined to take any action in support. Makarios therefore, despite his teachings as a priest, decided that perhaps Grivas was right after all, and that violence was the only way forward.

Therefore, at a meeting in January 1955, in the Bishop's Palace at Larnaca, Makarios and Grivas formed the organisation history now knows as EOKA - Εθνικι Οργανοσις Κυπριον Αγονιστον - Ethniki Organosis Kyprion Agoniston - National Organisation of Cypriot Freedom Fighters.

The birth place of EOKA. The palace of the Bishop of Kition, Larnaca, where in January 1955, Archbishop Makarios and George Grivas decided on violence rather than diplomacy. Larnaca Cathedral is on the extreme left.

THE EOKA CAMPAIGN

Armed insurrections obviously need arms, and in March and October 1954, arms had been tentatively smuggled into Cyprus on board the caique *Agios Georgios*. However when a third shipment was on its way in January 1955, the ship was intercepted by a Royal Naval patrol off the coast of Paphos. All the men on board were arrested and stood trial at Paphos in March, where large anti-British riots occurred during the court hearings.

Yet although the authorities suspected that violence was being threatened, the start of the campaign proper came as somewhat of a surprise. In the early hours of Friday 1 April 1955, bomb explosions occurred at various locations around the island, including government buildings and police stations. The Cyprus Broadcasting Station in Nicosia was stormed by armed raiders led by a certain Markos Dracos, and the radio transmitters destroyed. The first day of April 1955 is therefore seen as the start of the Liberation Struggle by the Greek Cypriots, and thus accounts for all the '1st April Avenues' and '1st April Roads' being found today in all the large towns on Cyprus.

And it was on 1 April, that the world first heard of EOKA, as notices appeared on walls and shop windows proclaiming that 'The Struggle for the Liberation of Cyprus has Begun'. These notices were signed by 'The Leader - Dighenis'. Dighenis was the nom-de-guerre adopted by Grivas in honour of a 10th century Greek hero, and which was his most well known nickname throughout the campaign; but he also was known to call himself 'The Leader' and sometimes 'The Uncatchable'.

The Cyprus Police were the natural first target, and so were subjected to bombing and shooting campaigns on police stations, intimidation, and threats of execution for any policeman not in sympathy with EOKA. The very first police officer to be murdered in the campaign was Police Sergeant Ioannis Demosthenous. At 2.30am on Wednesday 22 June 1955, PS Demosthenous was sitting typing in Amiandos police station. As the night was warm, the window was open. Suddenly, four masked men armed with machine guns, fired a burst through the window. PS Demosthenous was killed instantly. He left a widow and three daughters, and was buried in his home village of Mandria.

The violence escalated, and within nine weeks, three more police officers were dead. Special Constable Mikis Zavros, who was a postal clerk, was shot dead whilst on routine patrol in Nicosia on Wednesday 10 August; and just 18 days later, two more police officers suffered fatal injuries. Detective Constable Herodotias Poullis and Detective Constable Kotsiopoulos were on duty in Ledra Street, Nicosia, during a demonstration denouncing the forthcoming Lancaster Conference. Three youths jostled the officers whilst they were standing outside the Alhambra Hall market. Suddenly three shots were fired at point blank range, and both officers were killed instantly. Two of the youths escaped on bicycles, but the third, Michael Karaolis, was captured by horrified but quick-witted bystanders.

The reason for this, the so called Lancaster Conference, was an attempt to come to a solution of the crisis. Talks had been called for by the newly elected British Conservative Government under Prime Minister, Sir Anthony Eden. Held in Lancaster House, London, in August and September, these talks, however, finished in complete stalemate, and could reach no agreement between the leaders of Cyprus, Turkey and Greece.

And of course, not only police officers were being targeted by EOKA. In the seven months from the start of the campaign, no less than seven British military personnel had also been murdered. Following the collapse of the Lancaster Conference, coupled with increasing violence, the British answer was to send more troops to the island, accompanied by a recognised counter-terrorist expert. Replacing Sir Robert Armitage as Governor of Cyprus, Field Marshal Sir John Harding, had extensive military experience, and was at that time, the Chief of the Imperial General Staff.

However, this had the opposite effect - the violence increased dramatically. The British Institute in Nicosia was bombed, as well as the Nicosia and Famagusta Post Offices; and there were several riots after the trial of Michael Karaolis who had been sentenced to death for the murder of Constables Poullis and Kotsiopoulos. All this convinced Harding that EOKA was becoming better organised than at first thought, and so a State of Emergency was declared on Saturday 26 November 1955.

But not only that. Enosis and EOKA were receiving much more sympathy from the civil population, and it was clear that EOKA leaders were using civil disorder to pin down troops, so that guerrilla bands could have a free hand elsewhere. On one occasion, a large number of Cypriot schoolchildren rioted outside the Commercial Lyceum in Larnaca, and actually threw themselves, kicking, scratching and screaming at British troops, who were powerless to do anything.

Because of this development, it was obvious to the British Government that to deal with civil problems, the civil force - meaning the police force - must be strengthened. This view, however, had already been mooted by the Commissioner of the Cyprus Police himself.

Commissioner George Robbins had already visited London in early November 1955, and in talks with senior colleagues at New Scotland Yard, had sounded out proposals for a plan for experienced British police officers to be seconded to Cyprus. He had long suspected that the Cyprus Police had been heavily infiltrated and intimidated by EOKA sympathisers. The British Government agreed. And so, to provide an impartial police force, there seemed to be only one solution - send British police officers to the troubled island.

The first contingent of the Worcestershire County Constabulary to the UKU, ready to embark in December 1955. Seated in the centre is the 67 year old Chief Constable, Captain James Lloyd-Williams

THE UNITED KINGDOM POLICE UNIT TO CYPRUS

Eventually, 895 British policemen and women, all volunteers, were to serve on the United Kingdom Police Unit to Cyprus. The effect on the British police must have been tremendous. Most forces were struggling with the 'crime boom' of the 1950s (where reported crimes were rising at an average yearly rate of about 15 per cent), as well as being chronically under strength. To have to supply personnel to another country was a burden some forces could have done without, but the job had to be done, and the call went out for volunteers. The terms of agreement were simple: two years attachment consisting of 21 months residential service followed by three months leave.

By the autumn of 1955 the majority of the places were filled from an initially envisaged total of 150, and these flew out to Cyprus in late December, together with several police dogs and handlers. The police dogs were 'in action' first, as within days of arriving in Cyprus, they were sniffing out arms dumps in the Troodos Mountains.

The United Kingdom Police Unit (always referred to as the UKU, rather than UKPU) was sent as a supplement to the existing Cyprus Police, and not as a replacement. Integration, however, was easy, as Cyprus, being a British colony, had a police force organised along the traditional lines of the British Colonial Police.

The Commissioner (Mr C. George Robbins) and the higher ranking officers, were commissioned Colonial Police officers, whilst the rank and file were recruited from local personnel, both Greek and Turkish. However, when the UKU arrived in Cyprus, the British policemen moved up a rank from their British one. Thus a British Police Constable became a Police Sergeant, a British Police Sergeant became an Inspector, and a British Inspector became a Superintendent.

The uniform was of the standard pattern of the British Colonial Police. Summer uniform was khaki shirt and shorts with black peaked caps, black socks and black epaulettes. Winter uniform was 'police blue' high necked tunic and long trousers

The summer uniform of the UKU : khaki shirt and shorts; black peaked cap; black epaulettes; black socks

PS 2870 Peter Holyoak (Northamptonshire County Constabulary) wearing winter uniform, whilst on foot patrol in 'Murder Mile', Ledra Street, in the old, walled city of Nicosia

The main Headquarters in Nicosia. A Traffic Division Vauxhall Car is seen to the left, with the Cyprus Police badge on the driver's door

Inside the main Police Headquarters in Nicosia.

PS 2979 C. Wright, UKU, in winter uniform. PS Wright was a PC in the Metropolitan Police, and his tour of duty was from 15 August 1958 until 1 February 1959.

The Outstation at Agios Ioannis. These rural police stations were in charge of a UKU Sergeant, and were guarded by units of the British Army. Agios Ioannis is in the Commandaria Region of the Troodos Mountains, to the north of Limassol. The region is called the Commandaria because it was in the territory of the Knights Hospitallers whose Headquarters were at Kolossi Castle between 1291 and 1310 when they moved to Rhodes, and eventually Malta.

The Outstation in the village of Ora, in the eastern foothills of the Troodos Mountains. Today, it is the village coffee shop and restaurant. The building underneath the observation platform to the right, is a preserved block of stables, which is large enough to hold meetings of the local youth club.

Ktima, in effect, is in the northern outskirts of Paphos on the west coast. As such, it was one of the main centres for police and army operations for the western side of the island. This picture shows the main gate of Ktima Camp, with an Army Land Rover on the left, together with a UKU Land Rover containing two UKU Sergeants. The Cyprus Police badge is clearly visible on the driver's door.

On patrol in the foothills of the Troodos Mountains. These patrols consisted of Cypriot policemen accompanied by UKU officers. PS 2646 R. Tomlin (Kent County Constabulary) stands nonchalantly with his hand on the bonnet, with PC 650 Bekir Mehmet to his right. PC 1566 Houssein Mustafa leans on the nearside wing; and PC 1694 Houssein Mustafa is standing in the vehicle. Taking the photograph is PS 2756 P. Billinghurst (Metropolitan Police).

Reserve Units, or 'Riot Squads' were also formed to control civil unrest. These were comprised of Turkish Cypriot officers of the Cyprus Police, under the command of UKU Inspectors. This is Inspector 363 T. Matthews (Metropolitan Police), in summer uniform, who was in charge of Number 5, and later Number 12, Police Mobile Reserve Unit. Note the beret rather than the peaked cap

PC 473 Turhan Veli, Number 5 Police Mobile Reserve Unit, in riot gear, and riot equipment, in the 'attack' position

PC 658 Bekir Mehmet, Number 5 Police Mobile Reserve Unit, in winter uniform

In charge of the first contingent of the Unit to reach Cyprus in December 1955, was Detective Chief Superintendent Thomas Lockley, of the Staffordshire County Constabulary, which had also supplied 21 volunteers. Accommodation for the unit was normally in local hotels commandeered for the purpose in the large towns throughout the island. These hotels were under a 24 hour armed guard, which was always provided by the Turkish policemen of the Cyprus Police, alongside units of the British Army.

The day-to-day duties of the uniformed policemen of the Unit consisted of mobile patrols alongside the existing Cyprus Police, plus foot patrols inside the capital city of Nicosia; and duty as 'gaolers' at the detention centres. They were also fully armed at all times. The mobile patrols in Land Rovers had Cypriot drivers, with Cypriot policemen accompanied by British policemen. The foot patrols were also in groups.

There was also a Traffic Division, which used blue Vauxhall cars, with the Cyprus Police badge on the doors. Eventually a Marine Section was also formed, as well as Riot Squads consisting of Turkish Cypriot policemen under the command of UKU Inspectors.

The rural police stations, called Outstations, were placed in charge of UKU Sergeants, who were in command of the local policemen. These Outstations were always guarded by a contingent of the British Army.

As well as uniformed policemen, plain clothes officers of the Criminal Investigation Department (CID) and the Special Branch (SB), were present. Of necessity, the UKU was in close liaison with the police departments of the British armed forces on the island, who provided invaluable help against a common 'opponent'.

Unfortunately, the first contingent of the UKU were quickly reminded of the danger of the duty for which they had volunteered, because the Cyprus Police soon lost another officer murdered by terrorists. At 7.40am on Wednesday 11 January 1956, Detective Sergeant Abdullah Ali Riza was walking from his home to his police station in the village of Ktima, near to Paphos. As he was 50 yards from his home and 200 yards from his police station, he was shot in the back by a number of masked men. He suffered a wound to his right lung and another in his leg. Amazingly he managed to run after his assailants firing his own gun, but failed to hit any of them. He collapsed in the street, and died within minutes. He was 40 years old, married, with five children.

DS Riza was the first Turkish Cypriot police officer to be murdered, which was probably in retaliation for his part in a previous conviction of six EOKA members. Ironically, for his part in these convictions, he had just been awarded The Colonial Police Medal in the New Year's Honours List. Four youths were subsequently arrested for his murder.

And soon after, the fact that casualties of war are not always caused by the enemy, was brought home to members of the UKU by the tragic death of Superintendent Attfield. On Thursday 1 March 1956, the body of Superintendent Philip Stephen Attfield was found in a flat in Voulgar Voulgaroktinou Street, which is inside the old walled city of Nicosia. He had been shot with his own revolver.

Superintendent Attfield was not a member of the UKU, but was a commissioned Colonial Police officer, and had only been stationed in Cyprus since the previous October. He was 47 years of age, and had joined the Metropolitan Police in October 1928, serving until 1954. During the Second World War however, he was a Lieutenant Colonel in the Royal Military Police. On leaving the Metropolitan Police in 1954, he had rejoined the army, but eventually received a Commission into the British Colonial Police. The Inquest into his death recorded the verdict of suicide whilst in a state of severe depression.

And on the political front, things were changing - and changing drastically. On Saturday 10 March 1956, following his continued condoning of the violence by preaching sermons supporting the campaign, Archbishop Makarios was forcibly detained by the British Army at Nicosia Airport, whilst trying to board an aircraft bound for Athens. Members of his staff, including his Private Secretary, and Bishop Kyprianos of Kyrenia, were also detained. The Archbishop and his staff were flown out of Cyprus by the Royal Air Force, and a

The final resting place of Superintendent Philip Attfield in the British Cemetery in Nicosia. Superintendent Attfield was not of the UKU, but was a commissioned officer of the British Colonial Police. Tragically, he took his own life whilst in a state of severe depression in March 1956.

few days later, were all placed into exile on the island of Mahé in the Seychelles.

Not unnaturally, this so enraged the Greek Cypriots, that the EOKA campaign was stepped up. As a direct result, within the next nine months up to the close of the year, the incredible number of 19 police officers, five of them UKU members, would be murdered by EOKA gunmen. The first of these was just four days away, and was the first UKU member to be murdered.

PS 1683 Gerald Thomas Patrick Rooney, Kent County Constabulary, attached UKU

On Wednesday 14 March 1956, PS Gerald Rooney, aged 24, of the UKU, was on foot patrol in Ledra Street, Nicosia, with a Turkish Cypriot colleague of the Cyprus Police. Ledra Street is the main shopping street of the old town of Nicosia. It runs north from what was then called Metaxas Square (now called Eleftherias - 'Freedom' - Square, and which straddles the old city walls) into the maze of narrow streets of the old walled city, and thus there are many, many junctions with other streets and alleyways. Because of this, it was a favoured ambush place of the EOKA gunmen, as shots could be fired into Ledra Street from one of the side roads, with subsequent escape back into the maze of streets being made easy. And as such, pursuit was thus fairly impossible. Because of this, many murders and attempted murders were made in Ledra Street, which eventually caused it to be nicknamed 'Murder Mile'.

PS Gerald 'Paddy' Rooney died instantly, shot in the back, as he was on patrol in Ledra Street, at the junction with Hippocrates Street, trying to sort out a traffic entanglement. His Turkish Cypriot colleague, as well as a nearby civilian were both wounded.

Gerald Rooney was from the Kent County Constabulary and had been a Constable stationed at Chatham. He was however, an Ulsterman, being born in Ballycastle in County Antrim. His body was flown to England, and thence home to Northern Ireland, where he was buried with full honours in Saint Joseph's Church Cemetery, Culfeightrin, Ballycastle, on Monday 19 March 1956.

Ledra Street, Nicosia, the scene of the murder of PS Rooney, as it appears today. Hippocrates Street is to the right. In 1956, traffic was allowed in both streets, and PS Rooney was shot in the back as he attempted to disentangle a traffic jam at this junction. His Turkish Cypriot police colleague and a passer-by were wounded in the attack.

Saint Joseph's Church, Culfeightrin, Ballycastle, County Antrim, Northern Ireland. The final resting place of PS Gerald Rooney. Although a PC of the Kent County Constabulary, stationed at Chatham, Gerald Rooney was born in Ballycastle, and it was to Ballycastle he returned, aged 24.

It was at this point, after the murder of Gerald Rooney, that the British Government sent out to Cyprus a Commission to report on the state of the Cyprus Police. The Commission consisted of three senior police officers : Lieutenant Colonel Geoffrey White, Chief Constable of Warwickshire; Sir Henry Studdy, Chief Constable of the West Riding of Yorkshire; and Mr Francis Armstrong, one of HM Inspectors of Constabulary (and previously Chief Constable of Northumberland).

Just one week later, at 10.20 in the evening of Wednesday 21 March, PC Andreas Apostolides of the Cyprus Police, was drinking coffee in the local coffee shop in the village of Karavostasi, which is on the coast of Morphou Bay in the north west of the island. Suddenly a masked gunman walked in and shot PC Apostilides at point blank range. He died instantly.

Nine days later, Inspector Athanasis Stavrou was shot, on Friday 30 March. Wheeling his bicycle along a street in the Neapolis suburb of Nicosia, Inspector Stavrou was fired on by two gunmen. Although wounded, fatally as it turned out, he managed to fire five shots after the fleeing gunmen. But his wounds were far too great however, and he was to linger for over a week, before finally succumbing on Sunday 8 April. He was 45 years of age, married with three children. He was buried in his home village of Kazaphani.

Meanwhile, the clemency appeal of Michael Karaolis for the murder of Detective Constables Poullis and Kotsiopoulos, had been rejected by the Judicial Committee of the Privy Council in London. The expected reprisals were not long in coming, and would claim, within a couple of days, the Officer in charge of the Karaolis case.

Assistant Superintendent Kyriakos Aristotelous was a commissioned Colonial Police officer, who had been involved in the arrest and subsequent conviction of Karaolis. And his murder occurred in the most heart rending of circumstances.

Aristotelous was visiting the private Paraskevaides Clinic in Santa Rosa Street in Nicosia, where his wife had just given birth to their second child. At 5.25 on the afternoon of Sunday 15 April, he was talking to the doctor inside the doctor's office, when suddenly three men burst in, and eight bullets were fired. Aristotelous was hit and would die within minutes; the doctor was also wounded, but would survive. Kyriakos Aristotelous was 32 years old, having joined the Cyprus Police in 1942. Commissioned as an Assistant Superintendent in 1952, he had already been awarded The Colonial Police Medal.

On that same evening of the murder of Superintendent Aristotelous, Auxiliary PC Andreas Zanettos was watching a film in the cinema at Aradippou, which is just to the north west of Larnaca. Suddenly, an EOKA gunman fired three shots at close range. Two shots missed, but one wounded Auxiliary PC Zanettos in the stomach. He was rushed to Larnaca General Hospital, but he died later that evening. It has also to be mentioned that of the two bullets that missed the police officer, one wounded a 12 year old girl who was sitting close by.

Saint George's Day, Monday 23 April, saw riots and disturbances again in Nicosia, mainly this time, between Greek and Turk. A very violent confrontation occurred at the Ardath Tobacco factory's bonded warehouse, in Apti Chaoush Street, when gunmen opened fire, killing a Turkish employee.

Not unnaturally, hot-headed retaliation occurred, and a few hours later, at 1.30pm, shots were fired at a Greek Cypriot police officer. PC Hussein Nihat Vassif lived near to the Ardath factory, and on hearing this fresh outbreak of shooting, went outside.

Recognising the two men who had just fired the shots, he gave chase to them. He was in plain clothes, but was obviously known as a police officer. He managed to catch one of the men and fought with him trying to subdue him. The gunman's colleague, on seeing this, returned, and callously shot PC Vassif in the head. PC Vassif collapsed, but as he tried to get up, he was shot again at point blank range and died instantly.

Perhaps a small glimpse of sanity in all this lies in the fact that PC Vassif's murderer was captured at the scene by an act of supreme courage by a lady civilian. Mrs Emine Nevsat, a housewife, on hearing the shooting, came out of her house, and seeing the gunman fleeing the scene on a bicycle, actually chased after him and caught him. Jacovas Patasou, aged 22, eventually stood trial and was sentenced to death. PC Hussein Nihat Vassif was posthumously awarded the Colonial Police Medal for Gallantry, and Mrs Nevsat was awarded the British Empire Medal for Gallantry.

The reprisal murders for the failure of the Karaolis appeal continued. So much so, that Sir John Harding imposed strict curfews of motor vehicles in Nicosia, and closed places of entertainment. This strategy failed completely, and the riots and killings of British service personnel continued.

Michael Karaolis was finally hanged in the early hours of Thursday 10 May 1956, in Nicosia prison. As expected, widespread riots and disturbances occurred throughout the island, and in the following six weeks, the incredible number of 36 British servicemen, and three police officers were murdered by EOKA, including the second UKU officer.

Khrysokhou is a pleasant little village a couple of miles south of Polis. On the evening of Wednesday 23 May, PC Lisani Ahmed, was sitting in the village coffee shop, together with three other police officers, and the village Mukhtar (the Mayor). Suddenly, shots rang out and PC Ahmed was killed instantly, shot in the back. PC Ahmed was Turkish, and his murder sparked off anti-Greek riots amongst the Turkish community.

Just over a week later, at 7.30 am on Sunday 3 June, Special Constable Shadan Kara Ahmet Abdullah was shot dead in an ambush in Limnia village, just north of Famagusta. After this shooting, anti-Greek riots occurred in Famagusta, and at the funeral in Famagusta the day after, Greek commercial premises were fire bombed.

PS 1915 Reginald William Tipple, Metropolitan Police, attached UKU

And soon afterwards, the second officer of the UKU was murdered, on Thursday 21 June 1956. PS Reginald Tipple was a Constable of the Metropolitan Police, who was attached as a 'gaoler' on the police staff of the Pyla Detention Camp, which is about six miles north east from Larnaca. Wanting to buy a present for his five year old daughter, PS Tipple went into a shop near to Larnaca covered market place.

What happened next can be told in the words of EOKA themselves. Elenitsa Seraphim-Loizou was the only woman commander of EOKA, and was in charge of the Larnaca district. Her autobiography (*The Cyprus Liberation Struggle 1955-1959 : Through the eyes of a woman E. O. K. A. Area Commander*) has been translated into English, and quite naturally is extremely anti-British and pro-EOKA. It is full of imaginatively embroidered hearsay, and this is her description of that fatal day :

'The following day, another of our men, codename Erasmus, went into Kitieas' house, picked up the gun and headed for Ermou Street...Shortly afterwards a British officer (*sic : Seraphim, as she was not there, was guessing; she did not know that Tipple was of the UKU, and not the British Army*) accompanied by a Turk entered the market from the Eastern end. He was rather ostentatiously armed, but whenever he stopped to buy something he made an easy target. The fighter prepared to draw his gun, but then changed his mind. All around were people he knew. He decided that he would wait for the officer to leave the market. The Englishmen went on with his shopping unsuspectingly. There had not been any noteworthy E.O.K.A. activity in Larnaca, and he carried his gun out of habit.

Having purchased everything he wanted he made for the exit. His jeep *(sic)* was parked outside the china shop opposite. Erasmus followed him but before coming into range the man got into his jeep, start[ed] the engine and moved off in the direction of Zenonos Kitieos Street. The fighter decided to go in the same direction and find another target. On he went, glancing right and left, when suddenly he spotted the same officer at the photography store on the corner of Zenonos Kitieos Street and Evanthia Pieridou Street. The jeep was parked on the other side of the road. He stopped a few yards away from the jeep. Seconds after the Englishman came out of the shop and entered the jeep. Erasmus drew his gun and fired, hitting the officer in the temples. As he slumped to one side Erasmus took to his heels without firing a second bullet.'

The scene of the murder of PS Reginald Tipple as it appears today. Zenonos Kitieos Street, Larnaca, at the junction with Evanthia Pieridou Street, which is on the right.

Pyla Detention Centre, where PS Tipple was on the police staff, was about six miles north east of Larnaca. The temporary camp has long since been demolished, and the village of Pyla is now one of the main crossing points of the 'Green Line' which separates the Turkish north from the Greek south of the island.

The final resting place of PS Reginald William Tipple in the Kensington Cemetery, Uxbridge Road, Hanwell, London W7; Section 137, number 70

Reginald Tipple who was 32 years old, and a Londoner by birth, died within minutes on his way to hospital. His body was brought home and buried in the Kensington Cemetery, Hanwell, London.

On Monday 8 October, a certain Jacovou Tsardellis, a 22 year old grocer, was sentenced to death for the murder of PS Tipple. However, Seraphim-Loizou claims that Tsardellis was not the murderer of PS Tipple; he had been wrongly identified by an eyewitness. The identity of the real murderer, codenamed Erasmus, is not revealed in Seraphim-Loizou's book, all she says is that Erasmus and Tsardellis were remarkably similar in appearance, hence the mistake.

The EOKA campaign showed no signs of slackening, and after PS Tipple's murder, 50 more British policemen joined the UKU in Cyprus, bringing the total to nearly 200. Along with the extra police came a new Commissioner. On Monday 9 July 1956, Lieutenant Colonel Geoffrey White, who had been Chief Constable of Warwickshire since 1948, having had immense police experience in wartime Italy, took over command of the Cyprus Police from Mr George Robbins. Mr White had already been in Cyprus for the past four months, as a member of the Police Commission reporting on the state and morale of the Cyprus Police. This report would take another month to be published.

In the meantime, the tension on the island continued to rise, and soon another police officer was shot. Edward Charles Bonici Mompada was 28, a Maltese national, and Special Constable. His daytime job was as the Assistant Manager of a large store on Ledra Street.

After closing his shop at 5.00pm on Wednesday 25 July, Mompada was walking with his fiancée, Miss Drossoula Demetriadou. They walked down Ledra Street, turned into Hippocrates Street, and reached the corner with Thermopylae Street. Suddenly a shot rang out. Mompada had been shot in the back and died instantly. Miss Demetriadou was unhurt. Mompada had been murdered because he was a witness in the trial of a youth who had been charged with incitement during the riots following the execution of Karaolis.

In carrying the story, the *Cyprus Mail* included a photograph of the body lying in the street, with Miss Demetriadou standing shocked and forlorn beside it. It is one of the most heart rending pictures imaginable. It is even more shocking to realise that the photographer who took the picture was the murderer himself. Nicos Sampson was a journalist for the *Times of Cyprus,* who 'specialised' in shooting people in the back, and then taking a photograph of the body for newspaper publication.

No doubt because of her feelings, Miss Demetriadou later made a radio broadcast denouncing EOKA. Needless to say, the usual insanity prevailed, and her uncle was shot and killed a few days later.

The long awaited Police Commission Report was published on Tuesday 14 August. It had looked at the immediate history of the force, and the morale problems inherent with the EOKA campaign of intimidation. In all, the Report made six recommendations :

1. A government department should be formed, overseen by the Deputy Governor, which was to have responsibility of the Cyprus Police.
2. New and better scales of pay to be introduced to increase morale.
3. Specially designed police houses to be built.
4. A Police Cadet scheme to be started, recruiting from both Greek and Turkish communities.
5. The existing UKU in Cyprus to be used to train this hoped-for influx of recruits.
6. To do this, the UKU to be strengthened by another 100 British police officers.

Recommendations are easy to make, carrying them out however, is another thing. Certainly recommendation number six was put into place, but not before Special Constable Ali Hussein was shot dead on Tuesday 14 August, in the village of Agios Thomas, which is half way between Limassol and Paphos. His wife and young daughter were both injured, but survived.

PS 1913 Leonard Alfred Demmon QPM, Metropolitan Police, attached UKU
PS 1911 Maurice Eden GM, Metropolitan Police, attached UKU

On Friday, 31 August 1956, the UKU again suffered a fatality, in the so-called 'Battle of Nicosia Hospital'. Panaylotis Georgiou, a known member of EOKA, had been taken by two members of the Cyprus Prison Service to Nicosia General Hospital for an X-Ray. Accompanying them were two members of the UKU, PS Leonard Demmon, and PS Maurice ('Anthony') Eden. Hoping to rescue Georgiou, four EOKA members were waiting for the security party.

Following the X-Ray, the party passed through the crowded main hall of the hospital. Without warning, they were attacked by the waiting terrorists. Shots were fired at Demmon who collapsed, fatally wounded. PS Eden, armed only with a six-shot ·38 revolver, returned fire, killing two of the assailants. After expending his six shots, Eden grappled with another assailant, and hit him on the head with his empty revolver. He was then fired at by another EOKA gunman, who ran away, with Georgiou, and although PS Eden chased them both, they escaped. The 'Battle of Nicosia Hospital' had left four people dead : two terrorists; a Sergeant of the UKU; and a civilian hospital porter who had been caught in the crossfire.

PS Leonard Demmon, aged 24, was a Constable of the Metropolitan Police stationed at Orpington. His body was returned to England, and was buried in the churchyard of All Saints' Parish Church in Bark Hart Road, Orpington. For his actions on that day, he was subsequently awarded the Queen's Police Medal for Gallantry, a decoration now only awarded posthumously.

PS Maurice ('Anthony') Eden, also a Constable of the Metropolitan Police, was recommended for The George Medal. Tragically, however, on Monday 17 December, just one day before the confirmation in the *London Gazette* of his award, he was shot through the head with his own gun when, as he was bending down to pet a dog, the gun fell out of its holster onto the concrete floor causing it to go off.

His body was flown home to England, and he was buried in the New Southgate Cemetery in Brunswick Park Road, New Southgate, London.

The final resting place of PS Leonard Demmon, All Saints' Parish Church, Bark Hart Road, in Orpington, where he was stationed whilst serving with the Metropolitan Police.

The final resting place of PS Maurice Eden GM, New Southgate Cemetery, Brunswick Park Road, New Southgate, London; Section O number 623.

Trikomo is a village about a dozen miles north of Famagusta, with the police station in charge of PS Antony Hadjirousso. At 6.45am on the morning of Sunday 2 September 1956, PS Hadjirousso was on his way to his station. He was unarmed, and was walking through the Market Place. Suddenly a shot rang out, and PS Hadjirousso was killed instantly. He had 23 years police service to his credit, and was married with three children.

PS Cyril John Thoroughgood, Leicestershire and Rutland Constabulary, attached UKU

PS 2182 Hugh Brian Carter, Herefordshire County Constabulary, attached UKU

Just four weeks after the 'Battle of Nicosia Hospital', the UKU had to mourn two more members. On Friday 28 September 1956, PS Cyril Thoroughgood (Leicestershire and Rutland Constabulary), PS Hugh Carter (Herefordshire County Constabulary) and PS William Webb (Worcestershire County Constabulary) were in plain clothes in Ledra Street, Nicosia. They had been window shopping.

At the junction with Alexander the Great Street, three EOKA gunmen fired a volley of shots at the policemen and then disappeared into the maze of streets of the old walled city of Nicosia. Carter and Thoroughgood were killed instantly, both shot in the back, but Webb, although hit five times, survived. Again, the murderer was Nicos Sampson, and again he took a photograph of the scene, showing PS Carter and PS Thoroughgood lying on the pavement, with PS Webb, weapon drawn, in readiness for any more possible attacks.

The body of 25 year old PS Carter, was taken back to Herefordshire, and he was buried in the churchyard of Saint Michael and All Angels Parish Church in Lyonshall. PS Thoroughgood, however, remained in Cyprus, and he was buried in the British Cemetery in Kyriakou Matsi Avenue in Nicosia, the first member of the UKU to be so. Unfortunately, he would not be the last.

Ledra Street, Nicosia, at the junction with Alexander the Great Street, as it appears today, the scene of the murders of PS Cyril Thoroughgood and PS Hugh Carter, and the attempted murder of PS William Webb, by Nicos Sampson

The final resting place of PS Cyril Thoroughgood, in the British Cemetery in Nicosia.

PS Hugh Brian Carter, (Herefordshire County Constabulary)

(By kind permission of the family of PS Carter © West Mercia Constabulary

The final resting place of PS Hugh Carter, in the churchyard of Saint Michael and All Angels, Lyonshall, Herefordshire

(By kind permission of the family of PS Carter)

The front gate of the British Cemetery in Nicosia. The graves are well tended by the cemetery authority, and the key is readily available

It is with irony that the British Cemetery in Nicosia is in Kyriakou Matsi Avenue. It was not called by that name in 1956. In December 1958, Kyriakou Matsi, aged 32, was a wanted EOKA leader, who had been tracked down to a cellar hideout in the village of Kato Dikomo, half way between Nicosia and Kyrenia. Rather than surrender, Matsi had shot himself, before grenades had been thrown into the cellar by British soldiers. It was after the declaration of the Republic of Cyprus in 1960, that the street where the British Cemetery was located was renamed Kyriakou Matsi Avenue.

Nicos Sampson, the murderer of Sergeants Thoroughgood and Carter, fled to the safety of Saint Andrew's Monastery on the Karpasia peninsular at the north east of the island. However, despite a comprehensive manhunt, it was not until the following January (1957) that would be arrested in the village of Dhali.

However, before the arrest of Sampson in January 1957, four more police officers, three of them Special Constables, were to be murdered. On Monday 5 November 1956, PS Tassos Anastasiou was sitting in a coffee shop in the village of Akhna, which is half way between Larnaca and Famagusta. Suddenly, two masked gunman rushed into the shop and shot PS Anastasiou at point blank range; he died instantly. He left a widow and two children.

It is perhaps ironic to point out, that Alhna is now directly on the 'Green Line' between the Turkish north of the island, and the Greek south. As such, it has now been completely abandoned, leaving a ghost village, which is now patrolled by United Nations troops; it is forbidden to go there, or photograph there.

Alfred Stewart Hallam and John Victor Miles were both Directors of Astra Construction, and therefore employing several Greek Cypriot citizens. However, as they were both Special Constables, this seemed to make them 'legitimate' targets. On Thursday 15 November 1956, at 12.50pm, both men left their premises in Perdios Street, Nicosia, together.

No more than a few yards from their premises, they were both shot in the back by an EOKA murderer. Although both had revolvers, they had no time to use them because of the suddenness of the attack. Hallam, a married man with three children, died immediately. Miles however, also married, was seriously wounded, but despite being rushed to Nicosia General Hospital, would die six days later on Wednesday 21 November.

Jack Hadji-Ioannou was 22 and unmarried, and worked for the Cable and Wireless Company. He was also a Special Constable. At 1.00pm on Friday 21 December he was walking along 'Murder Mile', Ledra Street, Nicosia. On reaching the junction with Arsinoe Street, three shots were fired at him, by what witnesses later described as 'mere boys'. He collapsed, shot in the back, fatally wounded. Again, because of the suddenness of the attack, he did not have time to draw his revolver.

Politically of course, things had also been happening. Cyril, Baron (later Viscount) Radcliffe, a well respected Judge, had been appointed Legal Commissioner to Cyprus, with a view to making constitutional proposals, in an attempt to find a just settlement. Lord Radcliffe's report was published in December 1956.

All in all there were 15 proposals, but with the proviso that none should come into force until after the cessation of violence. However, at that point, changes *were* made to the naming of the Cyprus Police ranks. From henceforth, the chief officer would be termed a Chief Constable instead of Commissioner; Assistant Commissioners would become Assistant Chief Constables, and so on. It is hard to fathom the reason for this, except to speculate that by naming the new ranks in line with British domestic police forces, rather than the rank structure of the British Colonial Police, emphasis would therefore be put on the fact that the Cyprus Police was a *domestic* force rather than a *colonial* one.

Dhali is a large village mid-way between Larnaca and Nicosia. Following a tip-off, a private house was raided in the village on Thursday 31 January 1957. Inside was the much wanted man, Nicos Sampson, who was arrested by Superintendent Burge of the Cyprus Police, despite being fired at by Sampson.

Sampson appeared at a pre-trial hearing in Nicosia on Wednesday 13 March. PS William Webb of the UKU had no difficulty in identifying Sampson as the man who had murdered both PS Carter and PS Thoroughgood. When DS Jeffrey Leach (also UKU - Lancashire County Constabulary) was giving evidence of oral statements, where Sampson admitted being a member of EOKA and boasting of killing a number of policemen, Sampson interrupted the proceedings saying that any confession had been beaten out of him. However, this was refuted by evidence of medical examinations taken by independent doctors at Nicosia General Hospital soon after Sampson's arrest, which showed no marks of violence whatsoever.

At his trial proper, which started on Friday 26 April, Sampson again alleged he had been tortured, and yet again, evidence was produced that he had not. However, Sampson, although being identified by Webb, as the man who had murdered Carter and Thoroughgood, was acquitted of the murders because of procedural inadequacies. But, he was found guilty of possession of arms, and for firing at Superintendent Burge to resist arrest - and for those offences, he did receive the death penalty. Immediately, this provoked further outbreaks of violence, and the British took the expedient measure of commuting Sampson's sentence to life imprisonment, and flying him to England to serve his sentence there.

There was, during this trial, a distasteful episode. As is common when the defence has a weak or non-existent defence, it resorts to the oldest trick known to the legal profession - that of alleging 'police brutality', or in this case 'torture' - thus shifting the emphasis of the trial onto police procedure, rather than the guilt or innocence of the accused. As Sampson's confession was oral and not written, this is exactly what the defence resorted to.

A deputation of British politicians then arrived on the island in order to investigate the alleged torture of Sampson. Finding absolutely no evidence of this, but using the 'no smoke without fire' maxim, their subsequent report consisted of innuendo and unsubstantiated slurs against the British armed forces on the island, the Cyprus Police and the UKU in particular.

The resultant unpopularity of the deputation led to it being virtually ostracised until it left the island, and the leader of the deputation was left in no doubt as to the security forces' opinion of her. Even *The Times* in its leader of Wednesday 12 June 1957 shared this opinion :

'a large number of the police officers who are accused of such monstrous conduct are members of the UK police forces, whose traditions of restraint and humanity have long been the admiration of the civilised world, and it must appear unlikely that such men, with their years of training, should on arrival in Cyprus, apparently turn into typical members of Hitler's Gestapo, and on their return to the UK as quickly resume their well known and respected role'.

Meanwhile, in April 1957, Archbishop Makarios had been released from exile in the Seychelles, on the proviso that he did not return to Cyprus. So on Wednesday 17 April 1957, Makarios arrived in Athens to a hero's welcome, and immediately made an anti-British speech, confirming his insistence upon Enosis.

Also, at this point, the UKU was strengthened. The Cyprus Police had no women police officers, so to deal with the increasing incidences of female EOKA supporters being arrested, a contingent of 53 policewomen from 34 different United Kingdom forces, was sent. However, the UKU was soon to lose two more officers in separate, tragic, incidents, neither of which was because of terrorist activity.

PS 1738 William Edward Critchley, West Riding of Yorkshire County Constabulary, attached UKU

Married officers of the UKU had been allowed to bring wives and family with them if they wanted. PS William Critchley had done just that, arriving in July 1956, and the family lived in a flat in Nicosia. On Saturday 8 June 1957, PS Critchley was in the bedroom, playing with his revolver. Suddenly, the gun went off, killing him immediately. At the Inquest, the Coroner heard evidence from Mrs Critchley, and the suspicion of suicide was considered and dismissed. The verdict was 'death by accidental shooting'. PS Critchley was buried in the Nicosia British Cemetery in Kyriakou Matsi Avenue.

The final resting place of PS William Critchley, in the British Cemetery in Nicosia

PS Arthur James Coote (Durham County Constabulary)

(© By kind permission of the Chief Constable of Durham Constabulary)

The final resting place of PS Arthur Coote, in the British Cemetery,
Pano Polemidia, which is just to the north of Limassol

PS 1772 Arthur James Coote, Durham County Constabulary, attached UKU

On the day after the tragic death of PS Critchley, Sunday 9 June 1957, the UKU lost another officer. A UKU Land Rover carrying six officers, being driven along the Ktima to Polemi road, north east of Paphos, overturned into a ditch by the side of the road. PS Coote was killed instantly, but the other five officers escaped with minor injuries. Arthur Coote was 38 years old, and came from Roseworth, Stockton-on-Tees. Married with one child, PS Coote had joined the Durham County Constabulary in 1948, and had been in Cyprus since January 1956. He was buried in the British Cemetery at Pano Polemidia, north of Limassol, the only UKU officer to be so.

Having been freed by the British government, Archbishop Makarios renewed his agitation for Enosis, which naturally worried the Turkish Cypriots. Violence escalated on the island, as the Turkish Cypriot opposition to EOKA (the TMF - Turk Mudafa Teskilet - Turkish Defence Organisation) demonstrated their disappointment in the British administration by a series of street riots.

All the security forces, including the UKU, now had the task of keeping Turkish Cypriots away from Greek Cypriots, as well as suffering anti-British violence against themselves. But that did not stop the Cyprus Police still being subjected to violence.

On Saturday 9 November 1957, Inspector Mustafa Ahmed Beyaz, was driving along the Morfou to Nicosia road. With him in the car was his fiancée, Miss Fatima Hussein. They were going to Nicosia to discuss arrangements for their wedding. Suddenly, between the villages of Zodhia and Astromentis, just two miles to the east of Morfou, a lorry overtook them and forced them off the road. Two EOKA gunmen jumped from the lorry and opened up at point blank range. Inspector Beyaz was killed instantly, and although Miss Hussein was wounded, she survived. Inspector Beyaz was a training school instructor at the Cyprus Police Training School at Strovolos, a south western suburb of Nicosia.

And on the political front, changes were also happening. Field Marshall Sir John Harding was being replaced as Governor of Cyprus by Sir Hugh Foot, who arrived on Cyprus on Tuesday 3 December 1957. Obviously this was too good an opportunity to miss, and riots broke out all over the island, although soon subsiding. And just two weeks into the new year, the UKU lost another member, though again, not by terrorist action.

PS 2277 Charles Hector Brown, Cheshire County Constabulary, attached UKU

On Tuesday 14 January 1958, whilst driving a private car towards Limassol, PS Brown was in collision with a lorry in the village of Erimi, just three miles west of Limassol. Although taken to Limassol General Hospital, PS Brown died from his injuries in the early hours of Wednesday 15 January. Charles Brown, who was born in Penycae in Denbighshire, north Wales, was 30 years old, and had joined the Cheshire County Constabulary in 1951. He was buried in the British Cemetery in Kyriakou Matsi Avenue, Nicosia.

And to coincide with a new Governor, the Chief Constable was also replaced. Taking over from Lieutenant Colonel White, who had completed his two year attachment, Mr John E. S. Browne arrived in Cyprus in late January 1958. Mr Browne was 47 and had joined the Sheffield City Police aged 20. He had become the last Chief Constable of Scarborough Borough Police in 1944, continuing until 1947, when the force had been amalgamated with the North Riding of Yorkshire County Constabulary. He then served as Assistant Chief Constable of the North Riding before becoming Chief Constable of Nottinghamshire in 1949.

After the death of PS Brown in January, the year 1958 would see the deaths of five more police officers. One would be from the UKU, and four from the Cyprus Police.

Inspector Fred Raper was 59 years of age, and because of this was not placed on immediate 'active' service. Instead, he was employed as the Government Inspector of Detention Facilities. Inspector Raper died of natural causes on Saturday 8 March 1958, just a few days before the close of the Pyla Detention Centre near to Larnaca, and the transfer of inmates to the new Centre at Kokkinotrimithia, just six miles west of Nicosia. Inspector Raper was buried in the British Cemetery in Kyriakou Matsi Avenue, Nicosia.

Also not on 'active' duty because of age, 61 year old William Henry Louis Dear was attached to the Special Branch as an interrogator/interpreter. On Monday 14 April, at 11.10am, whilst walking in Aeschylus Street in Famagusta, he was shot in the stomach at close range. Although grappling with his assailants, he was mortally wounded, and staggered a few yards before collapsing. He would die the following day in Famagusta General Hospital.

William Dear, who came from Finchley in London, had been a British Colonial Police officer, with service in Malta before coming to Cyprus, and he was targeted because he was well known as a skilled interrogator. One of his suspected murderers was the projectionist of the Heraecay Cinema in Famagusta, which was promptly raided. Inside, an arms cache was found, which was destroyed in a controlled explosion, thus causing £50,000 worth of damage, much to the disgust of the owner of the cinema.

The month of June 1958 saw severe rioting. The Prime Minister of Turkey had welcomed the calls from the Greek Prime Minister for a NATO Permanent Council meeting to discuss the Cyprus situation. And in early June, a meeting in London proposed the 'Partnership Plan' put forward by Britain. Of course, by this time, any proposals would have been automatically rejected, irrespective of what those proposals were. And so it proved. The 'Partnership Plan' was rejected by both sides, resulting in the inevitable riots. During one riot in the Nicosia suburb of Kaimalki, at 5.30pm on Monday 9 June, Auxiliary PC Ahmet Hussein of the Cyprus Police was shot dead by unknown gunmen. During this particular riot, two other people had been killed, and four wounded.

The final resting place of PS Charles Hector Brown in the British Cemetery, Nicosia

The final resting place of Fred Raper in the British Cemetery in Nicosia

The British Cemetery, Nicosia, the final resting place of William Dear

In July 1958, the UKU was strengthened by a further 300 officers to combat the increasing violence, which would claim the next police victim within a matter of weeks. On Monday 1 September 1958, Assistant Superintendent Donal Thurston Murray Thomson was shot in the back as he was walking along 'Murder Mile'. Superintendent Thomson, a 35 year old New Zealander, was a commissioned officer of the British Colonial Police, stationed with the Cyprus Police.

It is believed that he was shot in retaliation against a judicial announcement which had been just made, clearing nine Turkish Cypriots of the 'Guenyeli Massacre' of June 1958. Seven Greek Cypriots had been murdered after having been mistakenly released from custody in the Turkish village of Guenyeli, just to the west of Nicosia.

PS 2850 Stanley Woodward, Durham County Constabulary, attached UKU

The last actual UKU officer to be murdered was PS Stanley Woodward of the Durham County Constabulary, who was killed in a carefully staged ambush high up in the Troodos Mountains near to Prodromos. On Monday 13 October 1958, he was on mobile patrol, when his Land Rover was ambushed with automatic fire directed towards vehicles from firing positions on both sides of the road. A mine was then detonated underneath his vehicle. PS Woodward was killed instantly. He was buried in the Nicosia British Cemetery, in Kyriakou Matsi Avenue.

Meanwhile, the world's politicians were seeking a solution, and after many meetings in London and Paris and the United Nations in New York, the Prime Ministers and Foreign Ministers of Turkey, Greece and Great Britain came together in Zurich in February 1959. A firm Declaration of Intent for the establishment of the Republic of Cyprus was agreed upon, and in London on Friday 20 February 1959 that agreement was actually signed. In effect, the agreement pointed the way forward to the establishment of the Republic of Cyprus, with the complete withdrawal of Britain as a colonial power. However, Britain was allowed to keep a military presence on the island at two Sovereign Base Areas, one at Akrotiri/Episkopi (near to Limassol); and one at Dhekelia (near to Larnaca).

The British Cemetery, Nicosia. The final resting place of Assistant Superintendent Donal Thomson

PS Stanley Woodward, Durham County Constabulary

(© By kind permission of the Chief Constable, Durham Constabulary)

The final resting place of PS Stanley Woodward, the British Cemetery, Nicosia

The final resting place of PS William Gillett, in the British Cemetery, Nicosia

Archbishop Makarios returned in triumph to Cyprus on Monday 2 March 1959 and would become the first President of the Republic of Cyprus in the following year. Colonel Grivas returned to Greece on Wednesday 18 March to a hero's welcome.

However things were not to be entirely peaceful for the birth of the new Republic. Enosis had not been achieved to the full extent that some EOKA members had wanted. Things therefore took some time to quieten down. Two last tragedies remained however.

PS 2539 William Sidney Gillett, Bristol City Police, attached UKU

The only UKU officer to die from natural causes, PS Gillett died from Leukaemia on Sunday 17 May 1959. He was buried in the British Cemetery in Nicosia.

And the last officer of the Cyprus Police to be murdered was PS Selim Mustafa, aged 38 of the Special Branch. Whilst refuelling his car at a garage in the Turkish quarter of Nicosia, another car pulled up. Two youths got out, and with a machine gun, sprayed shots at Mustafa, who was killed instantly. Twelve empty cartridge cases were found at the scene. This was the climax of several weeks of unrest in the Turkish community, although this murder may have been unconnected to the troubles, and may have been a personal 'score to settle'.

And it was probably Sergeant Mustafa's murder which indicated that peace would not return immediately. Splinter groups not wishing to lay down arms, coupled with the growing terrorist-unrelated criminality of gangs using the 'troubles' as a cover, plus the running-sore of sectarian violence, continued to be a problem. So much so, that the incoming Chief Constable designate of the new Republic of Cyprus Police, Chief Superintendent Hussein Hassabis, (who would take over on Thursday 1 October) reluctantly made the decision for the police to be routinely armed at all times.

But things were at an end for the United Kingdom Police Unit to Cyprus. The painful birth pangs of the infant Republic of Cyprus were just beginning, and in which the Unit would have no part; and the British police officers were gradually withdrawn back to their mother forces. Nearly 900 British policemen and women served on the Unit, and if they had been there longer than four months, each received the General Service Medal with 'Cyprus' clasp. Six policemen had been killed by enemy action, and nine wounded; four had died accidentally, one had died from natural causes, and 25 had been decorated.

The Queen's Birthday Parade of June 1959 provided the ideal opportunity for the 'Stand Down Parade', which occurred in the grounds of Ktima Hospital. Taking the salute was Mr G. Beresford, the District Commissioner, and officers of the UKU, as well as from the British Colonial Police, and the armed forces on the island, took part. However, for the UKU, just one more thing remained to be done.

As a mark of respect to all members of the UKU who died in the course of duty, a Memorial was dedicated at Saint Paul's Anglican Cathedral in Nicosia on Sunday 20 September 1959. The Memorial consists of a silver cross and two candlesticks. The Service of Dedication was attended by senior officers of the Cyprus Police and the UKU, and was conducted by the Archdeacon of Cyprus, the Venerable William Blackburn, assisted by the Anglican Archbishop of Jerusalem, the Most Reverend Angus MacInnes.

The silver cross is dedicated 'To all who gave their lives in the execution of their duty'. It stands on the High Altar of the Cathedral to this day.

June 1959, the Queen's Birthday Parade in the grounds of Ktima Hospital, Paphos, which was considered as the 'Stand Down' of the UKU. Taking the Salute is the District Commissioner, Mr G. Beresford.

The final march past of the UKU during the 'Stand Down', June 1959, at the Queen's Birthday Parade in the grounds of Ktima Hospital, Paphos

The west door of Saint Paul's Anglican Cathedral in Nicosia, a tranquil haven in the midst of a busy city, and ideal for the monument to the UKU

The reredos of Saint Paul's Cathedral, showing the usual position of the UKU Memorial Cross; with the Memorial Candlesticks in the niches either side.

The High Altar, with the Cross and Candlesticks placed for Services

The UKU Memorial Cross and Memorial Candlesticks in their position on the High Altar during Divine Worship

THE AFTERMATH

The political situation during these years in Cyprus was obviously far more complex than can be described here, and sadly Cypriot problems are by no means over. Detailed facts of Cypriot history of this period can be found elsewhere, but the bare-bones are these.

Trouble erupted soon after the establishment of the Republic of Cyprus, but this time the supplementary policing was given to an Australian and New Zealand Police Unit under the United Nations banner.

Archbishop Makarios continued to be the President of the Republic until ousted by a coup in July 1974. The new President was none other than Nicos Sampson, chosen as a puppet President by the Greek Junta Government. Archbishop Makarios escaped with his life and fled, ironically, to England.

Taking advantage of the unrest, Turkey invaded the north of Cyprus on 20 July 1974. When the dust had settled, Sampson was forced to resign on 28 July, afterwards being forever known as 'The Eight Day President'. Glafkos Clerides, the President of the House of Representatives was an interim President before Archbishop Makarios was re-instated as President in December 1974.

Archbishop Makarios died on 3 August 1977, and is buried high in the Troodos Mountains, near to Kykkos Monastery where he trained for the priesthood.

George Grivas had returned to Cyprus in 1964 to command the Cyprus National Guard. Being recalled to Greece in 1967 at the insistence of Turkey, Grivas secretly returned to Cyprus in 1971 and set up a political movement, ironically called EOKA-B, in direct opposition to Archbishop Makarios, his former ally. He died in January 1974, and is buried in Limassol. After his death, internal strife in EOKA-B caused a huge rift, with Archbishop Makarios publicly denouncing the movement. This action probably exacerbated the July 1974 coup against him.

Nicos Sampson was asked repeatedly by Archbishop Makarios to show repentance for his part in the coup of 1974, which put him into the Presidency. Sampson refused, and for his pains was sentenced to 20 years imprisonment in 1977. Two years later, however, he was released for medical reasons. He retired to France for the next eleven years before returning to Cyprus in 1990, to serve more of his sentence. He was released in 1993. Nicos Sampson died of cancer in May 2001, aged 66. He was buried in Nicosia.

Today, Cyprus is still divided into the Turkish Republic of North Cyprus and the Republic of Cyprus in the south. However, Cyprus is now policed by its own Greek Cypriot and Turkish Cypriot police, whilst the two British Sovereign Areas (Dekhalia near to Larnaca, and Akrotiri/Episkopi near to Limassol) are patrolled by the Sovereign Base Areas Police.

The United Kingdom Police Unit to Cyprus was the first ever such Unit to be constituted. The sacrifices it had to make were enormous, but the civilising influence of the British police model, operated by British police officers, was exactly what was needed for that stabilisation of everyday social life, without which, resolution of the problem would have been far and away more difficult. That was the nature of the task given to the UKU, and what was expected of it. And so well did it succeed, that on many occasions since, the tactic of supplying a UKU has been employed by the British Government in various 'trouble spots' around the globe: from Nyasaland to Grenada to Bosnia to Kosovo to Rhodesia.

The fact that this practice does indeed continue to this day, is testament to the excellence of the very first ever such Unit :

The United Kingdom Police Unit to Cyprus, 1955 to 1960.

The General Service Medal, with the 'Cyprus' clasp. This was awarded to all members of the UKU who had completed four months or more duty in Cyprus.

The medal on the right is the Police Long Service and Good Conduct Medal given for 22 years and above 'Exemplary Service' in the British civil police, which a significant number of the UKU would have gone on to receive in their home forces

The north end of Ledra Street, Nicosia, as it appears today, where it is abruptly cut short by the 'Green Line' which separates the Turkish north of the island, from the Greek southern part. The barricade is permanently manned by the Cypriot Army. The entrance to the left leads to the Paphos Gate which is permanently manned by United Nations troops. The monument in the centre is a sculpture which commemorates and laments the only divided capital city in the European Union

The south end of Ledra Street as it appears today, where it straddles the old city walls. In the 1950s, this was called Metaxas Square. Today, it is called Eleftherias ('Freedom') Square

To the British, the EOKA members were terrorists, and the period 1955 to 1960 was seen as a rebellion. But to the Cypriots, of course, it is seen as the Great Liberation Struggle from colonial rule. As such, it is looked upon with pride, and this newly completed National Liberation Museum, which is next to Saint John's Cathedral in Plateia Archiepiskopou Kyprianou in Nicosia, commemorates the period with many artefacts, documents and photographs

And not only is there a national museum, but there are also a number of local museums in the Cypriot villages. This one is at Sotira, which is in the eastern part of the island. It is just to the north of Agia Napa, which is now a favourite holiday spot for British tourists

And this local museum is in the grounds of Machairas monastery, in the foothills of the Troodos mountains. The museum, and this statue, commemorate Gregoris Afxentiou, who was the deputy commander of EOKA. In March 1957, Afxentiou and four men were besieged in nearby caves. Four surrendered to British forces, but Afxentiou refused, and was killed when explosives were used to collapse the roof of the cave.

The author is standing by the statue, to give some idea of the scale

During the EOKA uprising, quite naturally there were villages, especially in the Troodos Mountains, which were hideouts, and were considered safe from prying eyes and prattling tongues. One such village was Ora, in the foothills of the Troodos Mountains, about 25 kilometres north east of Limassol. It was to Ora that Petrakis Kyprianou fled after murdering a British civilian in Larnaca. Rather than surrender to British troops, he chose to shoot his way out, but was killed whilst doing so. Two statues to him are in Ora, together with this hillside memorial of 'EOKA' spelt out in white stones, which is visible for many miles

Not many signs of the period remain after 50 years. But this graffito appears to be from that time. It is in Georgiou Griva Digeni Avenue in Larnaca. A paint brush has been used, rather than a spray tin

However, the spirit of Enosis still lives on, despite the Greek Republic of Cyprus being economically and politically linked with Greece through common membership of the European Union. These graffiti, in Larnaca, are recent, as they were applied with a spray can rather than a brush. Note the EOKA shield in the top photograph

And EOKA hideouts are now on the tourist trail. This sign in the village of Lasania, 35 kilometres north east of Limassol, and well in the Troodos Mountains, was erected by the Ministry of Education and Culture, to mark the 'historical symbol' of these EOKA hideouts

APPENDIX 1

UNITED KINGDOM POLICE UNIT TO CYPRUS
1955-1960

NOMINAL LIST

Rank in Cyprus	Collar Number	Name	Date of Appointment	End of Service	Remarks
ABERDEEN CITY					
PS	2982	Laing, D.	5 Sep 58	4 Mar 59	
PS	2983	Hunter, D. C.	5 Sep 58	5 Dec 58	
PS	2987	Davidson, G.	5 Sep 58	4 Mar 59	
WPS	2388	McIntosh, M.	26 May 57	25 May 58	
ANGUS COUNTY					
Insp	193	Greig, J. J. T.	7 Mar 56	6 Dec 57	*Awarded the CPM*
PS	1878	Leslie, R.	7 Mar 56	24 Dec 59	
PS	2988	Mullin, H. W.	6 Sep 58	5 Dec 58	
PS	2985	Smith, R.	6 Sep 58	5 Dec 58	
BARNSLEY BOROUGH					
PS	2714	Gilmartin, D.	26 Jun 58	16 Feb 60	
BARROW IN FURNESS BOROUGH					
WPS	2389	Cromp, J.	26 May 57	30 Apr 59	
BEDFORDSHIRE COUNTY					
PS	2764	Hassall, K. A.	28 Aug 56	1 Nov 58	*Two tours*
PS	2153	Lloyd, J. E.	28 Aug 56	27 May 58	
PS	375	Davis, J. A.	4 Dec 57	3 Sep 59	
PS	2771	Roninan, D. M.	2 Aug 58	1 Feb 59	
PS	2772	Stanley, T. E.	2 Aug 58	1 Feb 59	
WInsp	418	Clapperton, M. C.	26 May 57	30 Apr 59	
WPS	2390	Childs, J. M.	26 May 57	26 May 58	

85

BERKSHIRE COUNTY
PS   2455   Barker, C. W.   3 Oct 57   2 Jul 59

BERWICK, SELKIRK AND ROXBURGH COUNTY
PS   1809   Dorward, G. D.   10 Jan 58   9 Oct 59

BIRKENHEAD BOROUGH

PS	2401	Jockes, J. P. L.	6 Jul 58	17 Feb 60
PS	2920	Light, R. W.	8 Aug 58	8 Nov 58
PS	2921	Cunchffe, J. H. F.	8 Aug 58	8 Nov 58
PS	2922	Brown, M.	8 Aug 58	8 Nov 58
PS	2923	Botting, B. H.	8 Aug 58	8 Nov 58

BIRMINGHAM CITY

Insp	551	Flanigan, J.	24 Sep 57	23 Jun 59	
PS	2458	Parsonage, R. G.	3 Oct 57	2 Jul 59	*Special Branch*
PS	2718	Whittington, P.	15 Jul 58	15 Feb 60	
PS	2831	Armstrong, C. J.	6 Aug 58	6 Nov 58	
PS	2832	Walker, J.	6 Aug 58	5 Feb 59	
PS	2833	Barrs, L. C.	6 Aug 58	5 Nov 58	
PS	2834	King, I. G.	6 Aug 58	5 Nov 58	
PS	2835	Jones, G. G.	6 Aug 58	5 Nov 58	
PS	2836	Pedlingham, A. N.	6 Aug 58	5 Nov 58	
PS	2961	Crawford, A, M.	15 Aug 58	14 Feb 59	
PS	2962	McIntosh, A. S.	15 Aug 58	14 Feb 59	
WInsp	478	Hands, M. M.	26 May 57	30 Apr 59	
WPS	2616	Morris, A.	26 May 58	30 Apr 59	
WInsp	419	Wren, P. E.	26 May 57	2 Jun 58	

BLACKBURN BOROUGH
WASP   Lovell, M. E.   20 May 57   1 May 59

BOLTON BOROUGH

PS	471	Lund, N.	7 Jan 58	6 Oct 59
PS	2636	Scoble, L. S.	28 May 58	16 Feb 60
PS	2640	Haslam, F. H.	28 May 58	16 Feb 60
PS	2924	Crimmins, C.	8 Aug 58	8 Feb 60
PS	2925	Moxom, A.	8 Aug 58	8 Feb 60
PS	2926	Freeman, P.	8 Aug 58	8 Feb 60
PS	2927	Holden, R.	8 Aug 58	8 Feb 60
PS	2928	Durie, D.	8 Aug 58	8 Feb 60

BRADFORD CITY

Insp	227	Dewhirst, K. C.	3 Jun 57	2 Mar 59	*CID*
PS	2469	Whitehouse, P. L.	12 Oct 57	11 Jul 59	*CID*
PS	2470	Peel, R.	12 Oct 57	11 Jul 59	*Special Branch*

PS	2944	Kershaw, J.	8 Aug 58	8 Feb 59
PS	2991	Stone, D. C.	11 Sep 58	10 Dec 58
WPS	2391	Bastow, F. J.	26 May 57	30 Apr 59
WPS	2392	Ibson, J. S.	26 May 57	25 May 58

BRISTOL CITY

Insp	353	Edwards, C. B.	28 Nov 56	27 Nov 58	
PS	2538	Hesking (Hosking?), A. K.	1 Nov 57	31 Jul 59	
PS	2539	Gillett, W.	1 Nov 57	17 May 59	*Died (Leukaemia)*
PS	722	Bruce, R. H.	25 Mar 59	22 Dec 59	
PS	2132	Kean, F. J.	7 Jun 58	17 Dec 59	
PS	2812	Wade, W. H.	6 Aug 58	6 Nov 58	
PS	2811	Crosbie, J.	6 Aug 58	5 Feb 59	
WPS	2393	King, K.	26 May 57	25 May 58	

BUCKINGHAMSHIRE COUNTY

PS	2138	Maydon, L. W. E.	24 Aug 56	27 May 58	
Insp	326	Brackett, L. M.	26 Sep 56	5 Jul 58	
PS	2878	Sheridan, J.	8 Aug 58	7 Nov 58	*CID*

CAMBRIDGE CITY

PS	2780	McClorg, W.	2 Aug 58	1 Nov 58
PS	2781	Tooke, G. F. F.	2 Aug 58	1 Nov 58
WPS	2617	Taylor, S.	26 May 58	30 Apr 59

CARDIFF CITY

PS	2467	Aslett, W. C. A.	12 Oct 57	11 Jul 59	*CID*
PS	2468	Mahoney, D. P.	12 Oct 57	11 Jul 59	
PS	2596	Griffiths, J. R.	18 Apr 58	16 Jan 60	
PS	2143	Wheakey, J. A. P.	7 Jun 58	16 Feb 60	
WPS	2394	Coke, J. M.	26 May 57	26 Feb 59	
WPS	2395	Hayes, P.	26 May 58	12 Jul 58	
WPS	2396	Mills, G. E.	26 May 58	25 May 58?	

CARLISLE CITY

| WPS | 2605 | Wilson, J. | 26 May 58 | 30 Apr 59 |

CARMARTHENSHIRE COUNTY

| PS | 2540 | Herbert, I. O. | 1 Nov 57 | 31 Jul 59 |

CHESHIRE COUNTY

PS	2272	Wilson, A. J.	26 Sep 56	17 Feb 60
PS	2273	Smethurst, J. V.	26 Sep 56	16 Feb 60
Insp	474	Burroughs, C. D.	26 Sep 56	15 Feb 60
PS	2275	Blackburn, J.	26 Sep 56	16 Feb 60
PS	2276	Denny, L.	26 Sep 56	15 Jul 58

PS	2277	Brown, C. H.	26 Sep 56	14 Jan 58	*Killed in Traffic Accident*
PS	2330	Mullane, D. F.	14 Oct 56	13 Jul 58	
PS	2368	Booth, W. E.	25 Apr 57	24 Jan 59	*Special Branch*
PS	2369	Broome, P. P.	25 Apr 57	15 Aug 57	*Resigned*
PS	2370	Taylor, D.	25 Apr 57	10 Dec 57	
PS	2371	Wakeman, J. C.	25 Apr 57	24 Jan 59	
PS	2711	Mort, K. E.	26 Jun 58	17 Apr 59	
PS	2942	Thompson, R. T.	8 Aug 58	8 Nov 58	
PS	2943	Keeman, J.	8 Aug 58	8 Nov 58	

CORNWALL COUNTY

PS	2145	Mathews, W. G. E.	28 Aug 56	27 May 58	
PS	2483	Hawkins, J. R.	4 Nov 57	3 Aug 59	
PS	2484	White, F. J.	4 Nov 57	3 Aug 59	*Special Branch*
PS	2706	Jenkin, M. D.	21 Jun 58	9 Feb 60	
PS	2816	Whatmore, D. J.	6 Aug 58	5 Feb 59	
PS	2817	Gibbs, J. S.	6 Aug 58	5 Feb 59	

COVENTRY CITY

PS	2161	Egglestone, J.	10 Apr 58	22 Jul 59
PS	2841	Linn, D.	6 Aug 58	5 Feb 59

CUMBERLAND AND WESTMORLAND COUNTY

Insp	225	Dougherty, J. C.	29 May 56	28 Feb 58
Insp	364	Tapping, C. F.	29 May 56	28 Feb 58
PS	1942	McMahon, M.	29 May 56	28 Feb 58
PS	1945	Rose, J. A.	29 May 56	28 Feb 58
PS	1944	Hutchinson, A.	29 Feb 56	28 Feb 58
Insp	544	Teasdale, T R.	29 May 56	16 Feb 60
Insp	528	Rigg, H. C.	29 May 56	16 Feb 60
ASP	259	Parkinson, J. E.	27 Aug 56	16 Feb 60
PS	2396	Dorran, M.	2 Jul 58	16 Feb 60
PS	2934	Jeffreys, B. F.	8 Aug 58	15 Feb 60

DENBIGHSHIRE COUNTY

WPS	2604	Jones, M. E.	26 May 58	30 Apr 59

DERBY BOROUGH

ACC	250	Burns, A.	11 Aug 56	27 Apr 58	*Awarded the CPM*
PS	2842	Todd, M. J.	6 Aug 58	5 Feb 59	

DERBYSHIRE COUNTY

Insp	560	Cuthbert, R.	26 Sep 56	16 Feb 60
PS	2271	Shaw, J.	26 Sep 56	15 Feb 60

PS	642	Parker, I. L.	4 Dec 57	3 Sep 59
PS	2847	Harley, H.	6 Aug 58	5 Feb 59
ASP	545	Bramley, J.	11 Sep 58	16 Feb 60

DEVONSHIRE COUNTY

Insp	554	Dowell, G. L. F.	31 May 56	15 Feb 60
Insp	529	Roper, D. J.	31 May 56	15 Feb 60
PS	2157	Libby, W. J. H.	28 Aug 56	15 Feb 60
WPS	2619	Backway, A.	26 May 58	30 Apr 59

DESWBURY BOROUGH

Insp	466	Hardman, C. B.	28 Nov 56	27 Aug 58
PS	2631	Walsh, J.	28 May 58	16 Feb 60
PS	2949	Carr, J. H.	8 Aug 59	8 Feb 59 (60?)

DONCASTER BOROUGH

| PS | 1704 | Witherington, K. T. | 24 Nov 57 | 23 Aug 59 |
| PS | 2967 | Holmes, R. | 15 Aug 58 | 14 Nov 58 |

DORSETSHIRE COUNTY

PS	2146	Edrich, W. G.	28 Aug 56	27 May 58
PS	2171	Heppell, C. B.	28 Aug 56	16 Feb 60
PS	2151	Walker, D. G.	28 Aug 56	27 May 58
PS	2158	Carey, G. W.	10 Apr 58	9 Jan 60
PS	2175	Roberts, D. A.	10 Apr 58	9 Jan 60
PS	2815	Geer, P. A.	6 Aug 58	5 Feb 59

DUDLEY BOROUGH

| PS | 2387 | Warren, W. | 9 Jul 58 | 16 Feb 60 |

DUMFRIES AND GALLOWAY COUNTY

| ASP | 194 | McCorkindale, H. | 7 Mar 56 | 16 Feb 60 |
| WPS | 2397 | Tulip, E. H. | 26 May 57 | 25 May 58 |

DUNBARTONSHIRE COUNTY

| Insp | 445 | McCormack, W. F. | 14 Oct 56 | 15 Feb 60 |

DURHAM COUNTY

ASP	178	Sparkes, J. H.	16 Jan 56	31 Oct 59	
Insp	476	Lancaster, H.	16 Jan 56	3 Oct 59	
PS	1770	Dunn, A. V.	16 Jan 56	15 Feb 60	
PS	1779	Lewis, J. W.	16 Jan 56	12 Feb 60	
PS	2980	Uden, A. L.	16 Jan 56	30 Nov 58	*CID, two tours*
PS	1774	Molony, F. R.	16 Jan 56	15 Oct 57	
PS	1776	Smith, J. D.	16 Jan 56	15 Oct 57	
PS	1781	Palmer, G. L.	16 Jan 56	17 Sep 57	

PS	1859	Willis, R.	25 Feb 56	24 Nov 57	
PS	1748	Cowell, J.	16 Jan 56	15 Oct 57	*Special Branch*
PS	2765	Anderson, F. J.	16 Jan 56	29 Jan 59	*Two tours*
PS	1772	Coote, A. J.	16 Jan 56	9 Jun 57	*Killed in Traffic Accident*
PS	1773	Earle, T.	16 Jan 56	15 Oct 57	
PS	1777	Jacobs, H. E.	16 Jan 56	3 Oct 59	*CID*
PS	1778	Longstaff, R.	16 Jan 56	15 Oct 57	
PS	1782	Dunn, J. J.	16 Jan 56	1 Feb 56	
Insp	236	Melvin, C. T.	25 Feb 56	24 Nov 57	
ASP	188	England, J. K.	25 Feb 56	24 Nov 57	*Awarded the CPM*
PS	2259	Joice, N.	26 Sep 56	25 Jun 58	*CID*
PS	2329	Johnson, C.	14 Oct 56	13 Jul 58	
PS	2374	Best, E. W.	26 Apr 57	25 Mar 58	
PS	2262	Wilson, V.	26 Sep 56	25 Jun 58	
Insp	458	Dawson, R.	26 Sep 56	25 Jun 58	
PS	2260	Ormston, A. C.	26 Sep 56	3 Jan 57	
PS	2532	Murray, A. J.	1 Nov 57	31 Jul 59	*CID*
PS	2533	Finlay, J.	1 Nov 57	31 Jul 59	*CID*
PS	2534	Smith, P.	1 Nov 57	31 Jul 59	
PS	2535	Embleton, S. J.	1 Nov 57	31 Jul 59	
PS	248	Brierly, J. C.	4 Dec 57	3 Sep 59	
PS	2639	Brown, J. G.	28 May 58	17 Feb 60	
PS	2641	Bainbridge, D.	28 May 58	16 Feb 60	
PS	2131	Sodder, W. L.	7 Jun 58	17 Feb 60	
Insp	532	Johnson, W. J.	15 Aug 58	17 Feb 60	
PS	2848	Coates, E.	6 Aug 58	5 Nov 58	
PS	2849	Dodds, J. R.	6 Aug 58	5 Nov 58	
PS	2851	English, E. G.	6 Aug 58	16 Feb 60	
PS	2852	Bell, R.	6 Aug 58	5 Feb 59	
PS	2853	Mullooly, W.	6 Aug 58	5 Feb 59	*CID*
PS	2854	Beetcham, K. P.	6 Aug 58	5 Nov 58	
PS	3001	Hall, H. T. G.	18 Oct 58	17 Apr 59	
PS	2850	Woodward, S.	6 Aug 58	3 Oct 58	*Murdered by EOKA*

EASTBOURNE BOROUGH

| PS | 1702 | Harmer, J. A. | 24 Nov 57 | 23 Aug 59 |
| WPS | 2601 | Storry, B. A. | 26 May 58 | 30 Apr 59 |

EAST RIDING OF YORKSHIRE COUNTY

| PS | 2263 | Taylor, J. | 26 Sep 56 | 25 Jun 58 |

EDINBURGH CITY

Insp	480	Gordon, G.	14 Oct 56	30 Dec 59
PS	1814	Ferrier, C. B. L.	31 Jan 58	30 Oct 59
PS	1815	Dawson, A. G.	31 Jan 58	16 Feb 60

PS	1842	Forsyth, E. T.	31 Jan 58	30 Oct 59	
PS	2997	Macdonald, D.	16 Sep 58	15 Mar 59	
PS	2998	Crawford, H. D.	16 Sep 58	15 Dec 58	
PS	2999	Torrence, W. T.	16 Sep 58	15 Dec 58	
PS	3000	Georgeson, S. J.	16 Sep 58	15 Dec 58	
WPS	2399	Johnson, M. H.	26 May 57	25 May 58	

ESSEX COUNTY

PS	1933	Morgan, E.	28 May 56	27 Feb 58	
PS	106	Simmons, D. B.	7 Jan 58	6 Oct 59	
PS	2145	Tuffin, D. F.	7 Jun 58	9 Feb 60	
PS	2146	Baddeley, F. A.	7 Jun 58	16 Feb 60	*Awarded the QCBC*
PS	2767	Mitchell, E. W.	2 Aug 58	1 Nov 58	
PS	2768	Butcher, D. A. T.	2 Aug 58	1 Nov 58	
PS	2769	Wilson, D. A.	2 Aug 58	1 Nov 58	
PS	2770	Scott, D. C.	2 Aug 58	1 Feb 59	
Insp	546	Batson, H. J.	11 Sep 58	19 Feb 60	

EXETER CITY

| WInsp | 420 | McKierman, C. | 26 May 57 | 2 Jun 58 | |

FIFESHIRE COUNTY

| PS | 2332 | Samuel, G. M. | 22 Jul 58 | 17 Feb 60 | |
| PS | 1811 | Gove, C. A. | 10 Jan 58 | 9 Oct 59 | |

FLINTSHIRE COUNTY

PS	510	Evans, D. D.	4 Dec 57	3 Sep 59	*Special Branch*
PS	2170	Palframan, A. K.	10 Apr 58	9 Jan 60	
WPS	2400	Bate, E. D.	26 May 57	26 May 58	

GATESHEAD BOROUGH

| PS | 2868 | Shanks, R. | 6 Aug 58 | 6 Nov 58 | |

GLAMORGANSHIRE COUNTY

Insp	221	Jones, B. J.	26 May 56	8 Mar 58	
Insp	222	Williams, D. E.	26 May 56	23 Aug 57	
PS	1931	Evans, C. H.	26 May 56	25 Feb 58	
PS	1930	Sault, M. T.	26 May 56	25 Feb 58	
PS	1928	Evans, A. J.	26 May 56	16 Feb 60	
PS	1934	Tomkins, F. I.	28 May 56	9 Feb 60	
PS	1935	Bowan, C. R.	28 May 56	27 Feb 58	
PS	2459	Egerton, T. G. N.	3 Oct 57	2 Jul 59	
PS	2460	Thomas, N. H.	3 Oct 57	2 Jul 59	*Special Branch*
PS	2594	Ashford, D. E.	18 Apr 58	27 Aug 59	
PS	2595	Gibson, C. J.	18 Apr 58	16 Feb 60	
PS	2715	Williams, J.	15 Jul 58	15 Feb 60	

PS	2818	Evarett, P. E.	6 Aug 58	5 Nov 58	
PS	2819	Johnson, L.	6 Aug 58	5 Nov 58	
PS	2820	Grant, C. G.	6 Aug 58	5 Feb 59	
PS	2821	Jones, A. G.	6 Aug 58	6 Dec 58	
PS	2822	Oliver, R. G.	6 Aug 58	5 Nov 58	
PS	2823	Davies, L. E.	6 Aug 58	5 Feb 59	
PS	2984	Phillips, R.	5 Sep 58	4 Dec 58	
PS	1929	Jones, R. A.	26 Mar 56	22 Nov 59	

GLASGOW CITY

Insp	425	Inglis, J. C.	25 Feb 56	23 Sep 59	
WInsp	415	Hunter, E.	20 May 57	19 May 58	

GLOUCESTERSHIRE COUNTY

PS	2163	Cook, J. A.	28 Aug 56	27 May 58	
PS	2162	Watts, R. J.	28 Aug 56	27 May 58	
PS	2537	Lightfoot, R. N.	1 Nov 57	31 Jul 59	*Special Branch*
PS	2400	Viles, C. J.	6 Jul 58	15 Feb 60	
PS	2813	Jeffries, C.	6 Aug 58	23 Aug 58	
PS	2814	Parris, S. W.	6 Aug 58	5 Nov 58	
PS	2960	Jones, G. J.	15 Aug 58	14 Feb 59	

GREENOCK BURGH

PS	2877	Johnstone, F. W. L.	25 Feb 56	2 Feb 59	*Two tours*

GRIMSBY BOROUGH

PS	2939	Foster, K.	8 Aug 58	8 Nov 58	
PS	2940	Ferguson, J. A.	8 Aug 58	8 Nov 58	

HALIFAX BOROUGH

SP	253	Buckley, T.	22 Aug 56	8 Aug 59	

HAMPSHIRE AND ISLE OF WIGHT COUNTY

PS	2141	Galpin, G. G.	28 Aug 56	16 Feb 60	
PS	2143	Rowsell, R. L.	28 Aug 56	27 May 58	
PS	2174	Taylor, P.	28 Aug 56	6 Jun 58	
PS	2150	Taylor, W. E.	28 Aug 56	27 May 58	
PS	2536	Austin, E. L.	1 Nov 57	31 Jul 59	
PS	2709	Neale, D. W.	26 Jun 58	16 Feb 60	
PS	2710	Colbourne, A. V.	26 Jun 58	15 Feb 60	
PS	2775	Pearce, F.	2 Aug 58	1 Feb 59	
PS	2776	Parry, T. M.	2 Aug 58	1 Feb 59	
WInsp	431	Stewart, M.	26 May 57	25 May 58	

HASTINGS BOROUGH

PS	2138	Knight, G. H.	7 Jun 58	20 Jun 59	

| WInsp | 2401 | Coles, J. E. | 26 May 57 | 30 Apr 59 | |
| WInsp | 479 | Tucknott, E. V. | 26 May 58 | 30 Apr 59 | |

HEREFORDSHIRE COUNTY

| PS | 2182 | Carter, H. B. | 28 Aug 56 | 28 Sep 56 | *Murdered by EOKA* |
| PS | 2717 | Roberts, S. | 15 Jul 58 | 16 Feb 60 | |

HERTFORDSHIRE COUNTY

WPS	2614	Lewis, K. L.	26 May 58	30 Apr 59	
WPS	2613	Ridley, J.	26 May 58	30 Apr 59	
WPS	2402	Cklarke, M. E.	26 May 57	26 Feb 59	
PS	2154	Pay, M. E.	28 Aug 56	12 Nov 56	
PS	2282	Eales, G. W.	26 Sep 56	16 Feb 60	
PS	2447	Sears, A.	13 Sep 57	12 Jun 59	
PS	2448	Pennicott, D. T.	13 Sep 57	12 Jun 59	
PS	2777	Sadler, F.	2 Aug 58	1 Nov 58	
PS	2778	McBride, D.	2 Aug 58	1 Nov 58	
PS	2779	Benton, J. D.	2 Aug 58	1 Feb 59	

HUDDERSFIELD BOROUGH

PS	2707	Large, J.	21 Jun 58	15 Feb 60	
PS	2968	Heley, R.	15 Aug 58	15 Nov 58	
WPS	2599	Boulter, M.	31 Dec 58	30 Apr 59	

ISLE OF ELY COUNTY

| PS | 2475 | Faulkner, J. | 15 Oct 57 | 14 Jul 59 | *Special Branch* |

KENT COUNTY

Insp	460	Herring, S. C.	14 Dec 55	17 Feb 60	
ASP	454	Poole, J.	14 Dec 55	16 Feb 60	
Insp	456	Foreman, C. J. D.	14 Dec 55	17 Feb 60	
Insp	162	Reynolds, R.	14 Dec 55	13 Jun 59	*CID*
ASP	161	Kirwan, F.	14 Dec 55	2 Sep 59	
Insp	472	Fraser, C. H.	31 Dec 55	19 Sep 59	*Awarded the CPM*
PS	1679	Stewart, R. A.	14 Dec 55	14 Jun 59	
Insp	235	Musgrove, L.	14 Dec 55	13 Sep 57	
ASP	160	Gosling, F. R.	14 Dec 55	13 Sep 57	
Insp	165	Gilmore, L. G.	31 Dec 55	30 Sep 57	
Insp	359	Dolphin, L. G.	14 Dec 55	13 Sep 57	*CID*
PS	1683	Rooney, G. T. P.	14 Dec 55	14 Mar 56	*Murdered by EOKA*
PS	1685	Briggs, L. S.	14 Dec 55	13 Sep 57	*Special Branch*
PS	1703	Hill, W. R.	31 Dec 55	30 Sep 57	
PS	1706	Knights, M. J.	31 Dec 55	30 Sep 57	*CID*
PS	2724	Whitcomb, G. E.	31 Dec 55	22 Oct 58	*CID two tours; Has published memoirs*

PS	2723	Perry, S. J.	31 Dec 55	22 Oct 58	*Two tours*
SP	85	White, A. H.	18 Feb 56	15 May 58	*Awarded the CPM*
PS	2456	Cortis, A. T.	3 Oct 57	2 Jul 59	*Special Branch*
PS	2457	Mitchell, E. G.	3 Oct 57	2 Jul 59	
PS	2598	Thomas, R. H.	18 Apr 58	16 Feb 60	
PS	2597	Hibben, J. F. A.	18 Apr 58	16 Feb 60	
PS	2647	Smith, G. M.	8 May 58	5 Feb 60	
PS	2646	Tomlin, R. J.	28 May 58	15 Feb 60	
PS	2648	Shenton, L. B.	26 Jun 58	8 Aug 58	
Insp	533	Miller, E. F.	15 Aug 58	16 Feb 60	

KINGSTON UPON HULL CITY

PS	2386	Fergus, L.	9 Jul 58	15 Feb 60	
WPS	2403	Hughes, M.	26 May 57	1 Jun 58	

LANCASHIRE COUNTY

PS	2766	Dent, A.	4 Jan 56	1 Nov 58	*Two tours*
PS	2729	Sloan, D.	4 Jan 56	16 Feb 60	*Two tours*
Insp	426	Sewart, A.	4 Jan 56	28 Oct 58	*Special Branch two tours; Awarded the CPM*
PS	1736	Chippendale, D. A.	4 Jan 56	3 Oct 57	
PS	1728	Bolton, A.	4 Jan 56	1 Oct 56	
PS	1720	Floyd, J. M.	4 Jan 56	3 Oct 57	*Special Branch*
Insp	566	Fahy, N. J.	4 Jan 56	16 Feb 60	*Awarded the BEM*
Insp	337	Livingstone, D. D.	4 Jan 56	3 Jul 59	
PS	1734	Kay, A.	4 Jan 56	3 Oct 57	
Insp	3005	Horsefall, J. H.	4 Jan 56	31 Oct 58	*Two tours*
Insp	172	Topping, E. J.	4 Jan 56	3 Oct 57	
Insp	171	Dawson, J.	4 Jan 56	3 Oct 57	
Insp	169	Brunskill, T. C.	4 Jan 56	3 Jul 59	*CID*
SP	170	Watkinson, T.	4 Jan 56	1 Oct 59	
PS	1723	Leach, J.	4 Jan 56	3 Oct 57	*Awarded the BEM*
ASP	168	Grundy, G.	4 Jan 56	1 Oct 59	
PS	1727	Mounsey, J.	4 Jan 56	3 Oct 57	*Special Branch; Awarded the BEM*
Insp		Beaham, J. J.	4 Jan 56	2 Jun 56	
Insp		Anderson, R. H. R.	4 Jan 56	16 Feb 60	
PS	1729	Kirwan, N.	4 Jan 56	3 Oct 57	
PS	1726	Dawson, J. P.	4 Jan 56	3 Oct 57	*CID*
Insp	475	Halsall, G. A.	4 Jan 56	1 Oct 59	
PS	1921	Harling, J. E.	11 Apr 56	10 Jan 58	*Special Branch*
Insp	365	Ball, H. M.	28 May 56	27 Feb 58	
PS	2476	Hardman, J.	15 Oct 57	14 Jul 59	*CID*
PS	2477	Garratt, K. E.	15 Oct 57	14 Jul 59	
PS	1937	Alton, L. S.	30 Dec 57	29 Sep 59	*CID*

PS	2633	Hipwell, G.	28 May 58	17 Feb 60
PS	2634	Snape, G. R. D.	28 May 58	17 Feb 60
PS	2635	Ingham, D. L.	28 May 58	16 Feb 60
PS	2397	Hatton, W.	6 Jul 58	14 Dec 58
PS	2398	Smith, R. D.	6 Jul 58	15 Feb 60
PS	2399	Pilcher, F. S.	6 Jul 58	15 Feb 60
Insp	534	Carline, S.	15 Aug 58	17 Feb 60
PS	2900	Graham, N.	8 Aug 58	9 Nov 58
PS	2901	Fearnley, G. S.	8 Aug 58	8 Feb 59
PS	2902	Turner, W. H.	8 Aug 58	8 Nov 58
PS	2903	Rice, L.	8 Aug 58	8 Feb 59
PS	2904	Stout, M. H. B.	8 Aug 58	8 Nov 58
PS	2905	Cocker, J. D.	8 Aug 58	8 Nov 58
PS	2906	Proctor, F. J.	8 Aug 58	8 Feb 59
PS	2907	Stuart, A. D.	8 Aug 58	8 Nov 58
PS	2908	Jackson, R. W.	8 Aug 58	8 Nov 58
PS	2909	Wood, J. N.	8 Aug 58	8 Nov 58
PS	2910	Hall, B.	8 Aug 58	8 Nov 58
PS	2911	Jones, A.	8 Aug 58	8 Nov 58
PS	2912	Roberts, A.	8 Aug 58	8 Nov 58
PS	2913	Fairclough, E.	8 Aug 58	8 Nov 58
ASP	257	Williams, C.	27 Aug 56	5 Jun 58
PS	3007	Hayes, T.	28 Nov 58	27 May 59
PS	3003	Smith, J. A.	31 Oct 58	30 Apr 59
WPS	2620	Roshton, N.	26 May 58	30 Apr 59
WPS	2404	Lown, J. M.	26 May 58	25 May 59

LEEDS CITY

Insp	431	Lawson, E.	3 Jun 57	3 Mar 59
PS	264	Conway, T.	4 Dec 57	3 Sep 59
PS	974	Pickering, J. E.	4 Dec 57	3 Sep 59
PS	2716	Cranage, R. A.	15 Jul 58	12 Feb 60
WPS	2609	Hunter, A.	26 May 58	30 Apr 59
WPS	2608	Jeffrey, B. R.	26 May 58	30 Apr 59
PS	2914	Taylor, K.	8 Aug 58	8 Nov 58
PS	2915	Hogg, S.	8 Aug 58	8 Feb 58
PS	2816	Curtis, J.	8 Aug 58	8 Nov 58
PS	2917	Shaw, D.	8 Aug 58	8 Nov 58
PS	2918	Forses, P. S.	8 Aug 58	8 Nov 58
PS	2919	Bebb, A. R.	8 Aug 58	8 Nov 58

LEICESTER CITY

PS	2075	Summers, B. D.	15 Feb 58	14 Nov 59
PS	2084	Whifield, J. F.	15 Feb 58	14 Nov 59
PS	2830	Pick, W. R.	6 Aug 58	5 Feb 58

LEICESTERSHIRE AND RUTLAND COUNTY

PS		Thoroughgood, C. J.	28 Aug 56	28 Sep 56	*Murdered by EOKA*
SP	270	Michael, G. A.	20 Sep 56	19 Jun 58	*Awarded the CPM*
ACC	247	Webster, J. R.	1 Aug 56	12 May 58	*Awarded the QPM*
PS	2481	Smith, L. A.	16 Oct 57	15 Jul 59	*CID*
PS	2882	Williams, T. D.	8 Aug 58	9 Feb 59	
PS	2989	Ball, P. H.	5 Sep 58	4 Dec 59	

LINCOLN CITY

PS	2464	Melton, J. E.	6 Oct 57	5 Jul 59	*Special Branch*
PS	2708	Duke, C. L.	21 Jun 58	16 Feb 60	
PS	2941	Waller, S. H.	8 Aug 58	8 Feb 59	

LINCOLNSHIRE COUNTY

Insp	552	Flatman, B. P.	26 Sep 56	16 Feb 60	
PS	2280	Piercy, A. H.	26 Sep 56	5 Jul 58	
PS	2281	Shaw, W. J. W.	26 Sep 56	5 Jul 58	
PS	2331	Drakes, J. W.	14 Oct 56	15 Jul 58	
PS	2279	Martin, D. S.	26 Sep 56	12 Feb 57	
Insp	451	Camamale, J. H.	20 Nov 57	19 Aug 59	*CID*
PS	2703	Fletcher, R.	20 Jun 58	17 Feb 60	
PS	2935	Wright, A. S.	8 Aug 58	8 Nov 58	
PS	2936	Galvin, E. G.	8 Aug 58	8 Feb 59	
PS	2937	Dickinson, K. W.	8 Aug 58	8 Feb 59	
PS	2938	Fleming, A. E.	8 Aug 58	8 Nov 58	
PS	3002	Green, J. W. C.	18 Oct 58	17 Apr 59	

LIVERPOOL CITY

PS	2089	Murray, D. J.	26 Sep 56	5 Jul 58	
PS	2088	Mercer, J. D.	26 Sep 56	4 Jul 57	
PS	2090	Fray, W. R.	26 Sep 56	4 Jul 57	
PS	2091	Flynn, M.	26 Sep 56	25 Jun 58	
SP	271	Williams, A.	29 Sep 56	19 Jun 58	
ASP	427	Muat, F.	3 Jun 57	2 Jun 59	*CID*
PS	2945	Jones, R.	8 Aug 58	8 Feb 59	
PS	2946	Smith, G. A.	8 Aug 58	3 Feb 59	
PS	2947	Green, W.	8 Aug 58	8 Nov 58	
PS	2948	Nickson, J. J.	8 Aug 58	8 Aug 59	

CITY OF LONDON

PS	2758	Brown, J. P.	2 Aug 58	1 Feb 59	
PS	2759	Dunstan, I. G.	2 Aug 58	1 Feb 59	
PS	2760	Lee, J. A.	2 Aug 58	1 Nov 58	
PS	2761	Newton, E. G.	2 Aug 58	1 Nov 58	
PS	2762	Wilson, J. W.	2 Aug 58	1 Mar 59	
PS	2763	Ayres, J. G.	2 Aug 58	1 Nov 58	

PS	2970	Martin, P. T.	15 Aug 58	14 Feb 59	
PS	3006	McAfee, F.	19 Nov 58	9 May 59	

METROPOLITAN POLICE

Insp	183	Bearne, R. S.	11 Feb 56	10 Nov 57	*CID;*
					Awarded the CPM
Insp	184	Clive, E	11 Feb 56	9 Sep 56	
ASP	185	Pinhey, E.	11 Feb 56	16 Feb 60	*Awarded the CPM*
Insp	186	Stanton, J. T. D.	11 Feb 56	16 Feb 60	
Insp	187	Thomason, D. E.	11 Feb 56	10 Nov 57	
ASP	455	Herlihy, J. M.	11 Feb 56	31 Jan 60	*Awarded the CPM*
Insp	348	Rollo, J. A.	11 Feb 56		*Awarded the BEM*
PS	1854	Woodmore, R. A.	11 Feb 56	10 Nov 57	*CID*
PS	1845	Willard, G. A.	11 Feb 56	10 Nov 57	*Special Branch;*
					Awarded the BEM
PS	1846	Fersbury, E. E.	11 Feb 56	10 Nov 57	
PS	1847	O'Day, T.	11 Feb 56	10 Nov 57	
Insp	512	Bunce, C. J.	11 Feb 56	10 Aug 59	
Insp	540	Brister, S. H. D.	11 Feb 56	12 Feb 60	*Awarded the BEM*
Insp	557	Clinker, A. R.	11 Feb 56	19 Feb 60	
PS	1851	Russ, A. E.	11 Feb 56	16 Feb 60	
PS	1852	Bartlett, F. W.	11 Feb 56	30 Mar 57	
Insp	362	Mathews, M. J.	11 Feb 56	20 Dec 58	
A/ASP	360	Cooper, P. R.	11 Feb 56	16 Feb 60	
Insp	363	Mathews, T. J.	11 Feb 56	16 Feb 60	
Insp	331	Holderness, E. V. D.	11 Feb 56	16 Feb 60	
Insp	349	Parker, L.	11 Feb 56	9 Feb 60	
ASP	398	Peasley, J. T.	7 Dec 55	20 Nov 60	
ASP	224	Green, J. H.	28 May 56	17 Feb 60	
Insp	109	Hall, N. W.	7 Dec 55	7 Jun 56	
PS	1673	Liddell, J.	7 Dec 55	7 Jun 56	
PS	1674	Beverly, A. J.	7 Dec 55	7 Jun 56	
PS	1675	Edwards, D. F.	7 Dec 55	7 Jun 56	
PS	1677	Lindenburn, C. J.	7 Dec 55	7 Jun 56	
PS	1783	Wells, T. E.	19 Jan 56	19 Jul 56	
PS	1784	Taylor, G. W.	19 Jan 56	19 Jul 56	
PS	1801	Richards, E. G.	19 Jan 56	19 Jul 56	
PS	1802	Lotz, J. W. M.	18 Jan 56	19 Jul 56	
PS	1803	Metcalfe, J. W.	18 Jan 56	15 Sep 56	
PS	1804	Inde, W. G.	18 Jan 56	19 Jul 56	
PS	1936	Blythe, L.	27 May 56	16 Jul 56	
PS	1937	Honniball, D. W.	27 May 56	27 Nov 56	
PS	1938	Pinney, K. E. A.	27 May 56	27 Nov 56	
PS	1939	Higgs, R. D. E.	27 May 56	27 Nov 56	
SP		O'Donnell, T. H.	5 Mar 56	16 Sep 56	
Insp	192	Thomas, R. G.	5 Mar 56	4 Dec 57	

PS	1867	Card, C. A.	5 Mar 56	15 Feb 60	
PS	1868	Gash, R.	5 Mar 56	16 Feb 60	
PS	1869	Forbes, A. F.	5 Mar 56	15 Feb 60	
Insp	457	Devereux, D. K.	5 Mar 56	16 Feb 60	
Insp	333	Warrior, J. H	5 Mar 56	4 Sep 59	
PS	1872	Paine, J. E.	5 Mar 56	31 Jul 56	
PS	1873	Russell, V. W.	5 Mar 56	4 Dec 57	
PS	1874	Trudgill, L. C.	5 Mar 56	16 Feb 60	*CID*
PS	1875	Drinkwater, E. C.	5 Mar 56	4 Dec 57	
PS	1876	Titmarsh, W. A.	5 Mar 56	4 Dec 57	
PS	1877	Cross, S. W.	5 Mar 56	21 Dec 59	*Special Branch*
Insp	201	Kevern, W. C.	5 Mar 56	21 Dec 57	
PS	1909	Lancaster, K. L.	28 Mar 56	18 Dec 56	
PS	2725	Exley, R.	28 Mar 56	28 Jan 59	*Two tours*
PS	2727	Krebbs, L. N. P.	28 Mar 56	1 Nov 58	*Two tours*
PS	1911	Eden, M.	28 Mar 56	17 Dec 56	*Awarded the GM; Killed in shooting accident*
PS	1912	Stead, R.	28 Mar 56	13 Dec 56	
PS	1913	Demmon, L. A.	28 Mar 56	31 Aug 56	*Murdered by EOKA; Awarded the QPM*
PS	1914	Marshall, H. L.	28 Mar 56	21 Dec 57	
PS	1915	Tipple, R. W.	28 Mar 56	21 Jun 56	*Murdered by EOKA*
PS	1916	Tempest, G. M.	28 Mar 56	19 Feb 60	
PS	1917	Straiton, W. J.	28 Mar 56	31 Dec 57	
PS	1918	McKay, D.	28 Mar 56	16 Oct 56	
PS	2131	Wheeler, E. L.	17 Aug 56	31 Dec 57	
PS	2132	Davidson, A. T.	18 Aug 56	17 May 58	
PS	2133	Wilson, D. B.	18 Aug 56	13 Sep 57	
PS	2134	Potter, G. L.	18 Aug 56	5 Jul 58	
PS	2137	Hackett, H.	28 Aug 56	27 May 58	
PS	2130	Edwards, E. P.	17 Aug 56	16 Feb 60	
PS	2135	Evans, R.	18 Aug 56	17 Feb 60	
PS	2129	Roberts, L. O.	17 Aug 56	19 Feb 60	
PS	2136	Kerston, A. D.	18 Aug 56	9 Feb 57	
Insp	556	Ashton, G. W.	10 Nov 57	9 Aug 59	
PS	2446	Hills, J. P.	13 Sep 57	12 Jun 59	*CID*
PS	2440	Cooper, L. G.	13 Sep 57	12 Jun 59	*Special Branch*
PS	2442	Wilson, D. E.	13 Sep 57	12 Jun 59	*Special Branch*
PS	2441	Eves, H. R. H.	13 Sep 57	22 Jun 59	*Special Branch*
PS	2443	Kirby, W. F.	13 Sep 57	16 Feb 60	
PS	2465	Seignior, J. A.	13 Oct 57	12 Jul 59	*Special Branch*
PS	2542	Hill, K. J.	10 Nov 57	25 Jun 59	
PS	2544	Cook, A. B.	10 Nov 57	17 Jul 59	*Special Branch*
PS	2545	Cluer, F. E.	10 Nov 57	9 Aug 59	
PS	2541	Utley, D. B.	10 Nov 57	16 Feb 60	

PS	1933	Wheatley, B. L.	11 Mar 58	10 Dec 59
PS	1942	Yates, J.	11 Mar 58	10 Dec 59
PS	1935	Keane, P. T.	11 Mar 58	10 Dec 59
PS	1944	Truhol, C. S.	11 Mar 58	10 Dec 59
PS	1952	Brighton, L. T. C.	11 Mar 58	15 Feb 60
PS	1945	Kemp, P. J.	11 Mar 58	10 Dec 59
PS	2026	Bainbridge, M. G.	11 Mar 58	10 Dec 59
SP	562	Butler, P. K. J.	22 Oct 58	11 Nov 58
ASP	563	Vibart, P. J.	22 Oct 58	11 Nov 58
PS	2730	Gregory, J. L.	2 Aug 58	1 Nov 58
PS	2731	Maclenna, C. A.	2 Aug 58	1 Nov 58
PS	2732	Reynolds, A.	2 Aug 58	1 Nov 58
PS	2733	Acteson, C. G.	2 Aug 58	1 Nov 58
PS	2734	Herbert, R. F.	2 Aug 58	1 Feb 59
PS	2735	Burnett, E. M.	2 Aug 58	1 Feb 59
PS	2736	Richardson, D.	2 Aug 58	1 Nov 58
PS	2737	Bradnun, W. R.	2 Aug 58	1 Nov 58
PS	2738	Bourne, K.	2 Aug 58	1 Feb 59
PS	2739	Kent, P. C.	2 Aug 58	1 Nov 58
PS	2740	Stobart, R. M.	2 Aug 58	1 Nov 58
PS	2741	Turner, A. P.	2 Aug 58	1 Feb 59
PS	2742	Tremlett, A. J.	2 Aug 58	1 Feb 59
PS	2743	Cheston, A. G. S.	2 Aug 58	1 Feb 59
PS	2744	Peskett, C. M.	2 Aug 58	1 Feb 59
PS	2745	Martin, I. M.	2 Aug 58	1 Feb 59
PS	2746	Jones, J. G.	2 Aug 58	1 Nov 58
PS	2747	Cheetham, J. M.	2 Aug 58	1 Feb 59
PS	2748	Forder, J.	2 Aug 58	1 Nov 58
PS	2749	Meakings, J. H. L.	2 Aug 58	17 Feb 60
PS	2750	Gladwell, K. S. A.	2 Aug 58	1 Nov 58
PS	2751	Wright, R. A.	2 Aug 58	1 Feb 59
PS	2752	Waller, I. D.	2 Aug 58	1 Nov 58
PS	2753	Champler, N. P. G.	2 Aug 58	1 Nov 58
PS	2754	Norris, J. P.	2 Aug 58	16 Feb 60
PS	2755	Hunter, R. C.	2 Aug 58	16 Feb 60
PS	2756	Billinghurst, P.	2 Aug 58	16 Feb 60
PS	2757	Lawrie, R. L.	2 Aug 58	1 Feb 59
PS	2979	Wright, C. J.	15 Aug 58	1 Feb 59
PS	2990	Little, C. D.	5 Sep 58	4 Dec 58
SP	191	Chapman, T. H.	5 Mar 56	18 Dec 56
WPS	2627	Burgess, J.	26 May 58	30 Apr 59
WPS	2377	Burgess, J. A.	26 May 57	30 Apr 59
WPS	2626	Coueney, J.	26 May 58	30 Apr 59
WPS	2622	Dale, A.	26 May 58	30 Apr 59
WPS	2380	Farrant, D.	26 May 57	30 Apr 59
WPS	2381	Ford, S. J.	26 May 57	30 Apr 59

WPS	2625	Harrison, P.	26 May 58	30 Apr 59	
WPS	2623	Niven, J.	26 May 58	30 Apr 59	
WPS	2624	Petherick, P.	26 May 58	30 Apr 59	
WPS	2385	Pole, M.	26 May 57	30 Apr 59	
WPS	2629	Rogerson, S.	26 May 58	30 Apr 59	
WPS	2628	Sandell, E.	26 May 58	30 Apr 59	
WSP	413	Barker, W. T.	20 May 57	19 Nov 58	*Awarded the CPM*
WPS	2376	Barnes, A.	26 May 57	26 May 58	
WPS	2378	Chandler, B.	26 May 57	3 Sep 58	
WPS	2377	Treanor, R.	26 May 57	25 May 58	
WInsp	43	Reeve, O. M.	26 May 57	25 Feb 59	
WPS	2383	Louett, S.	26 May 57	25 Feb 59	
ASP	416	Partridge, J. M.	26 May 57	25 May 58	
WInsp	417	McIntyre, M.	26 May 57	25 May 58	
WPS	2384	Manley, R. E.	26 May 57	25 May 58	
WPS	2382	Gobby, P.	26 May 57	25 May 58	
WPS	2379	Dennison, M.	26 May 57	25 May 58	

MIDDLESBROUGH BOROUGH

PS	2865	Watson, K.	6 Aug 58	6 Nov 58	
PS	2866	Huggins, R.	6 Aug 58	6 Nov 58	
WPS	2405	Yates, E. L.	26 May 57	2 Jun 58	

MID WALES COMBINED

Insp	447	McCormick, F.	28 Aug 56	15 Feb 60	

MONMOUTHSHIRE COUNTY

PS	2170	McDonald, W. J. A.	28 Aug 56	25 Aug 57	
PS	2445	Rowlands, H. G. P.	13 Sep 57	12 Jun 59	
PS	2449	Lewis, G. W.	13 Sep 57	12 Jun 59	

MONTGOMERYSHIRE COUNTY

Insp	450	Simmonds, C. R.	28 Aug 56	16 Feb 60	*CID*

MOTHERWELL AND WISHAW BURGH

WPS	2406	Macpherson, B.	26 May 57	30 Apr 59	

NEWCASTLE ON TYNE CITY

Insp	358	McGregor, C. H.	3 Dec 57	12 Sep 58	
PS	1289	Borland, C. B.	6 Dec 57	5 Sep 59	
PS	2137	Cuthberton, W. D.	7 Jun 58	15 Feb 60	
PS	2388	Howstan, B. T.	11 Jul 58	16 Feb 60	
PS	2390	Duncan, A.	11 Jul 58	16 Feb 60	
PS	2333	Urwin, H.	22 Jul 58	15 Feb 60	
PS	2885	Beattie, S. W.	8 Aug 58	8 Nov 58	
PS	2886	Duncan, G.	8 Aug 58	2 Mar 59	

PS	2887	Trotter, L.	8 Aug 58	8 Nov 58	

NEWPORT (MONMOUTHSHIRE) BOROUGH

PS	2879	Bevan, E. P. K.	8 Aug 58	8 Feb 59	
WInsp	2407	Preece, C. A.	26 May 57	30 Apr 59	

NORFOLK COUNTY

PS	2139	Irwin, M. J.	28 Aug 56	27 May 58	
PS	2167	Luke, B.	28 Aug 56	27 May 58	
PS	2791	Dye, J. O.	2 Aug 58	1 Feb 59	
PS	2792	Buttle, C. J.	2 Aug 58	1 Nov 58	
PS	2793	Goodrum, M. S.	2 Aug 58	1 Nov 58	
PS	2974	Smith, J. E.	15 Aug 58	14 Feb 59	

NORTHAMPTON BOROUGH

PS	2828	Cockrum, R.	6 Aug 58	6 Nov 58	
PS	2829	Warner, C. W.	6 Aug 58	6 Nov 58	

NORTHAMPTONSHIRE COUNTY

PS	2179	Oakenson, J. A.	28 Aug 56	6 Jun 58	
PS	2176	Russell, R. D.	28 Aug 56	6 Jun 58	
PS	2178	Pell, T. A.	28 Aug 56	27 May 58	
SP	254	Willey, R.	17 Aug 56	16 May 58	*Awarded the CPM*
PS	2869	Watson, R.	6 Aug 58	5 Feb 59	
PS	2870	Holyoak, P.	6 Aug 58	5 Feb 59	
WPS	2603	Keaveny, M. M.	26 May 58	30 Apr 59	

NORTHUMBERLAND COUNTY

Insp	244	Blackburn, J. J.	16 Jul 56	15 Apr 58	
Insp	245	Hornby, J.	16 Jul 56	15 Apr 58	
Insp	361	Hindmarsh, E. P.	16 Jul 56	15 Apr 58	
Insp	448	Jackson, J. E.	16 Jul 56	16 Feb 60	*Awarded the CPM*
PS	4063	Maville, E. N.	16 Jul 56	15 Feb 60	
PS	2064	Turnbull, R. L.	16 Jul 56	15 Apr 58	
PS	2062	Hill, S. M.	16 Jul 56	15 Apr 58	
PS	2258	Pearson, S. B.	26 Sep 56	25 Jun 58	
A/ASP	325	Hindmarsh, G. P.	26 Sep 56	16 Feb 60	
PS	2644	Poland, W.	28 May 58	16 Feb 60	
PS	2280	Kennedy, W. A.	15 Oct 57	14 Jul 59	*Special Branch*
PS	2650	Lynch, M. T.	28 May 58	1 Nov 58	
PS	2642	Mcnab, A.	28 May 58	15 Feb 60	
PS	2331	Elliott, N.	22 Jul 58	17 Feb 60	
Insp	535	Cattermole, C. C.	15 Aug 58	15 Feb 60	*CID*
PS	2857	Green, J. N.	6 Aug 58	15 Feb 59	
PS	2858	Brown, J.	6 Aug 58	5 Nov 58	
PS	2859	McGregor, M. I.	6 Aug 58	5 Feb 59	

PS	2860	Lander, D.	6 Aug 58	5 Nov 58
PS	2861	Simpson, G.	6 Aug 58	16 Feb 60
WPS	2621	Meadows, R. M.	26 May 58	30 Apr 59
WPS	2408	Patterson, E.	26 May 57	25 May 58

NORWICH CITY

PS	1703	Allatson, R. G.	24 Nov 57	23 Aug 59
PS	2701	Thackeray, D.	20 Jun 58	16 Feb 60
PS	2783	Ross, N.	2 Aug 58	2 Nov 58
PS	2784	Hooper, D. A.	2 Aug 58	7 Sep 58

NOTTINGHAM CITY

ASP	356	Easter, C. H.	28 Nov 56	27 Aug 58	
ASP	429	Oates, A. W.	3 Jun 57	2 Mar 59	*CID*
PS	1179	Smith, H. D.	4 Dec 57	3 Sep 59	
PS	439	Camm. L.	25 Mar 58	22 Dec 59	
PS	2794	Terry, J.	2 Aug 58	1 Nov 58	
PS	2795	Berridge, J.	2 Aug 58	1 Nov 58	
PS	2796	Hulland, M. R.	2 Aug 58	1 Feb 59	

NOTTINGHAMSHIRE COUNTY

Insp	226	Hines-Wragg, J. H.	30 May 56	16 Feb 60	
Insp	227	Dewhirst, J. F.	30 May 56	29 Feb 58	
PS	1946	Richardson, C. H.	30 May 56	16 Feb 60	
PS	1947	Layton, L. J.	30 May 56	16 Feb 60	
PS	1955	Le-Bor, K.	30 May 56	26 Nov 59	
PS	1952	Ogden, E.	30 May 56	28 Feb 58	
PS	1954	Coaten, H. G.	30 May 56	16 Feb 60	
PS	1951	Dunning, G. D.	30 May 56	16 Feb 60	
ChCon		Browne, J. E. S.	15 Feb 58	29 Sep 59	*Awarded the QPM*
ACC	471	Smalley, J.	11 May 58	10 Feb 60	
PS	2444	Cotterill, J.	13 Sep 57	12 Jun 59	*Special Branch*
PS	2139	McLean, R. W.	7 Jun 58	16 Feb 60	*CID*
Insp	539	Whitehead, J.	28 Aug 58	16 Feb 60	*CID*
PS	2825	Showtall, D. A.	6 Aug 58	17 Feb 60	
PS	2826	Margerison, J.	6 Aug 58	5 Nov 58	
PS	2827	Thompson, M.	6 Aug 58	5 Feb 59	
PS	2951	Jarvis, A. J.	15 Aug 58	14 Feb 59	
PS	2952	Howe, A. W.	15 Aug 58	14 Feb 59	
PS	2955	Levick, D. D.	15 Aug 58	14 Feb 59	

OLDHAM BOROUGH

Insp	357	Kirkman, H.	28 Nov 56	27 Nov 58	*Special Branch*
PS	2972	Tunnicliffe, B.	15 Aug 58	15 Nov 58	

OXFORD CITY

PS	2805	Boxall, E. H.	6 Aug 58	6 Nov 58
PS	2806	Dent, A. C.	6 Aug 58	6 Nov 58

OXFORDSHIRE COUNTY

PS	2804	Halford, N. F.	6 Aug 58	5 Feb 59

PAISLEY BURGH

PS	2992	Jones, W. H.	11 Sep 58	10 Mar 59

PERTH AND KINROSS COUNTY

PS	2986	Stewart, J. D.	5 Sep 58	4 Mar 59

PLYMOUTH CITY

Insp	354	Sharp, P. J.	28 Nov 56	27 Aug 58	*CID; Awarded the CPM*
PS	2463	Jennings, T. B.	4 Oct 57	3 Jul 59	*CID*
PS	2800	Jones, E. F.	8 Aug 58	8 Nov 58	
PS	2801	Wright, G. A.	8 Aug 58	8 Nov 58	
WInsp	2606	Phillips, K. M. M.	26 May 58	30 Apr 59	
WPS	2607	Meese, F. J.	26 May 58	30 Apr 59	
WPS	2409	Vosper, I.	26 May 57	2 Jun 58	

PORTSMOUTH CITY

ACC	248	Saunders, H. M.	1 Aug 56	1 Sep 58	
ASP	355	Richardson, F. W.	28 Nov 56	16 Feb 60	
Insp	434	Walters, D. A.	26 Jun 57	21 Nov 59	*CID*
PS	641	Orchard, A. J.	4 Dec 57	3 Sep 59	
PS	1454	Pegden, R. E. T.	25 Apr 58	24 Jan 60	
PS	2807	Shaw, W. B.	6 Aug 58	6 Nov 58	
PS	2808	Bowskill, A. D.	6 Aug 58	5 Feb 59	
WPS	2615	Chandler, M. A.	26 May 58	30 Apr 59	

PRESTON BOROUGH

PS	2959	Duncan, W.	15 Aug 58	14 Feb 59
WPS	2602	Midgley, R. M.	26 May 58	30 Apr 59

READING BOROUGH

PS	2546	Church, M. A.	10 Nov 57	9 Aug 59
PS	2702	Hall, K. E.	20 Jun 58	3 Dec 58
PS	2773	Stanford, J.	2 Aug 58	1 Nov 58
PS	2774	Titmuss, B. A.	2 Aug 58	1 Nov 58
WSP	477	Timberlake, J.	20 May 58	1 May 59

RENFREW AND BUTE COUNTY

ASP	189	Taylor, A. J.	25 Feb 56	12 Nov 59	*Awarded the CPM*

PS	1866	Teasdale, H. A.	25 Feb 56	24 Nov 57
Insp	542	Macdonald, E.	25 Feb 56	16 Feb 60
PS	2994	Hendry, P.	12 Sep 58	11 Mar 59
PS	2995	Johnston, J.	12 Sep 58	11 Dec 58
PS	2996	Stewart, R.	12 Sep 58	11 Mar 59

ROCHDALE BOROUGH

CSP	251	Saunders, G. T.	7 Aug 56	6 May 58
PS	2382	Hinningam, R. A.	9 Jul 58	16 Feb 60
PS	2384	Hamer, A. R.	9 Jul 58	16 Feb 60
PS	2973	Pollitt, E.	15 Aug 58	14 Nov 58

ROTHERHAM BOROUGH

PS	2964	Davis, C. L.	15 Aug 58	14 Feb 59
PS	2965	Sawson, G. A.	15 Aug 58	15 Nov 58
PS	2966	Scott, F.	15 Aug 58	15 Nov 58
PS	1849	Hepworth, J. E.	11 Sep 58	15 Feb 60
WInsp	2410	Brearly, M. R.	26 May 57	30 Apr 59

SCOTTISH NORTH EASTERN COUNTIES

PS	2334	Tough, K. J.	14 Oct 56	13 Jul 58
PS	2993	Thompson, A. W.	12 Sep 58	11 Mar 59

SHEFFIELD CITY

Insp	428	Healy, M.	3 Jun 57	2 Mar 59	*CID*
PS	2462	Barton, K. J.	3 Oct 57	2 Jul 59	*Special Branch*
PS	2466	Murphy, P. J.	3 Oct 57	2 Jul 59	*Special Branch*
PS	2975	Fox, A.	15 Aug 58	14 Feb 59	
PS	2976	Savage, L.	15 Aug 58	14 Feb 59	
WPS	2411	Maltby, I.	26 May 57	30 Apr 59	
PS	2977	Burroughs, R.	15 Aug 58	15 Nov 58	
PS	2978	McGhee, M.	15 Aug 58	15 Nov 58	

SHROPSHIRE COUNTY

PS	2839	Morris, L. S.	6 Aug 58	6 Nov 58
WPS	2600	Foster, A. J.	26 May 58	30 Apr 59

SOMERSETSHIRE COUNTY

WPS	422	Hunt, J. M.	26 May 57	26 Feb 59

SOUTHAMPTON BOROUGH

PS	2172	Quenault, F. F.	10 Apr 58	17 Feb 60
PS	2785	Mitchell, H.	2 Aug 58	1 Feb 59
PS	2786	Trenchard, R. A.	2 aug 58	1 Feb 59
PS	2787	Mason, J. A.	2 Aug 58	1 Nov 58
PS	2788	Quinn, B. M.	2 Aug 58	1 Jun 59

PS	3004	Holloway, J. C.	31 Oct 58	29 Apr 59	

SOUTHEND BOROUGH

PS	2473	Cundy, A. A.	15 Oct 57	3 Nov 58	
PS	2474	Wilkin, F. W. J.	15 Oct 57	31 Aug 58	
PS	1746	Enright, J. J.	8 Sep 58	16 Feb 60	
PS	2789	Widdicombe, E. C.	2 Aug 58	1 Nov 58	
PS	2790	Kirley, W. L.	2 Aug 58	1 Nov 58	

SOUTHPORT BOROUGH

ACC	71	Rowbottom, R. E.	29 Nov 55	28 Aug 57	*Awarded the QPM*

SOUTH SHIELDS BOROUGH

PS	2855	Dial, J. W.	6 Aug 58	6 Nov 58	
PS	2856	Tait, H.	6 Aug 58	16 Feb 60	

STAFFORDSHIRE COUNTY

ASP	182	Wright, H.	1 Feb 56	31 Oct 57	*CID; Awarded the CPM*
Insp	179	Bentley, C.	1 Feb 56	31 Oct 57	*CID*
Insp	347	Simpson, H. G.	1 Feb 56	31 Oct 57	*CID*
ASP	181	Cumpston, T. L.	1 Feb 56	19 Oct 59	
ASP	180	Fullerton, S.	1 Feb 56	31 Oct 57	
Insp	281	Jones, W. L.	1 Feb 56	19 Oct 59	*Awarded the MDS*
Insp	346	Gidwell, J. H.	1 Feb 56	31 Oct 57	
Insp	2720	Bryers, M. J.	1 Feb 56	15 Nov 58	*Two tours*
PS	1814	Jordan, F. L.	1 Feb 56	31 Oct 57	
PS	1806	Guest, J.	1 Feb 56	31 Oct 57	
PS	2722	Fanshaw, G. H.	1 Feb 56	15 Feb 60	*Two tours*
PS	1815	Waller, H. L.	1 Feb 56	18 Oct 57	
PS	1808	Skellan, J.	1 Feb 56	31 Oct 57	*CID*
PS	1807	Spencer, J. J.	1 Feb 56	21 Sep 58	
Insp	555	Wright, H. L.	1 Feb 56	16 Feb 60	
PS	1807	Gregg, M.	1 Feb 56	13 Mar 56	
ACP	82	Lockley, T.	31 Dec 56	1 Oct 57	*Awarded the OBE*
Insp	260	Lupton, H.	28 Aug 56	8 Apr 57	
ASP	271	Pegg, R. A.	28 Aug 56	16 Feb 60	
Insp	449	Beardmore, J. A.	28 Aug 56	6 Jun 58	
PS	2164	Boshell, B. A.	28 Aug 56	27 May 58	
PS	2149	Wallace, J. W. (J. D.?)	28 Aug 56	6 Jun 58	
PS	538	Harris, J. G.	4 Dec 57	3 Sep 59	
PS	2637	Birch, S.	28 May 58	16 Feb 60	
PS	2638	Harvey, H.	28 May 58	16 Feb 60	
Insp	558	Simpson, H. G	31 Oct 58	15 Feb 60	*CID*
PS	2837	Austin, J.	6 Aug 58	6 Nov 58	
PS	2838	Jones, J. F.	6 Aug 58	6 Nov 58	

PS	2884	Mellor, B.	8 Aug 58	8 Nov 58	
WPS	2610	Allen, J.	26 May 58	30 Apr 59	
WPS	2618	Wakelin, J.	26 May 58	30 Apr 59	
WPS	2412	Smeaton, M.	26 May 57	25 May 58	

STIRLINGSHIRE AND CLACKMANNANSHIRE COUNTIES

PS	1862	Middler, S.	25 Feb 56	24 Nov 57	*Special Branch*
PS	1861	Fleming, M.	25 Feb 56	24 Nov 57	*Special Branch*
PS	1860	Macleod, M. I. S.	25 Feb 56	24 Nov 57	*Special Branch*
PS	1920	Garden, A.	11 Apr 56	10 Jan 58	
PS	1657	Officer, J.	10 Jan 58	16 Feb 60	

STOCKPORT BOROUGH

PS	2929	Sheldrake, M.	8 Aug 58	14 Feb 59	
PS	2930	White, D. A. W.	8 Oct 58	19 Nov 59	
PS	2931	Bruckshaw, D. I.	8 Aug 58	8 Feb 59	

STOKE ON TRENT CITY

PS	204	Bailey, T.	4 Dec 57	3 Sep 59	
PS	2630	Wooton, G. E.	18 May 58	16 Feb 60	
PS	2846	Roper, D. F. C.	6 Aug 58	6 Nov 58	

EAST SUFFOLK COUNTY

PS	2134	Potter, R. W.	28 Aug 56	27 May 58	*Special Branch*
PS	2451	Field, R.	3 Oct 57	16 Feb 60	
PS	2452	Hopes, E.	3 Oct 57	16 Feb 60	
PS	2453	Peters, S. A.	3 Oct 57	2 Jul 59	*CID*
PS	1931	Newman, G. K. J.	11 Mar 58	10 Dec 59	
WPS	2398	Wheeler, H. M.	26 May 57	25 May 58	

WEST SUFFOLK COUNTY

| PS | 2454 | Ambrose, C. R. | 3 Oct 57 | 2 Jul 59 | *Special Branch* |

SUNDERLAND BOROUGH

| PS | 2867 | Knowles, R. | 6 Aug 58 | 5 Feb 59 | |

SURREY COUNTY

Insp	543	Cox, S. E.	28 Aug 56	16 Feb 60	*CID*
Insp	459	Healk, T. B.	28 Aug 56	16 Feb 60	
PS	2147	Newman, B. W.	28 Aug 56	27 May 58	
PS	2159	Rosher, R. H.	28 Aug 56	16 Feb 60	
PS	2177	Swain, A. P.	28 Aug 56	27 May 58	
PS	2332	Bevan, J. A.	14 Oct 56	13 Jul 58	
PS	2372	Scrimshaw, J. A.	15 Apr 57	16 Feb 60	
PS	2797	Kingsford-Curran, R. J.	2 Aug 58	1 Nov 58	
PS	2798	Hewitt, B. G. W.	2 Aug 58	1 Nov 58	

PS	2799	Farndale, T. C. S.	2 Aug 58	1 Feb 59
PS	2800	Alden, A. B.	2 Aug 58	16 Feb 60
PS	2801	Ryder, F.	2 Aug 58	1 Nov 58
PS	2802	Bartlett, R. T. W.	2 Aug 58	1 Feb 59
PS	2803	Mitchell, R.	2 Aug 58	1 Feb 59

EAST SUSSEX COUNTY

PS	2180	Carrigan, J. W.	28 Aug 56	16 Feb 60
PS	2155	Davies, J. A.	28 Aug 56	15 Feb 60
PS	2156	French, A. P.	28 Aug 56	15 Feb 60
PS	1930	White, T. J.	11 Mar 58	10 Dec 59
PS	2395	Shoesmith, K. A.	2 Jul 58	16 Feb 60
PS	2971	Maywood, S.	15 Aug 58	14 Nov 58

WEST SUSSEX COUNTY

ASP	262	Post, E. H.	28 Aug 56	16 Feb 60	
Insp	444	Brooks, C. J.	28 Aug 56	16 Feb 60	
PS	2173	Gowland, R. H.	28 Aug 56	27 May 58	
Insp	527	Holin, E.	28 Aug 56	16 Feb 60	*Awarded the MDS*
PS	2643	Ewans, E. S.	28 May 58	15 Feb 60	
PS	2645	Vye, L. C. E.	28 May 58	16 Feb 60	
PS	2649	Tinkler, A. E.	28 May 58	16 Feb 60	
PS	2547	Norman, D. A.	5 Sep 58	15 Feb 60	
PS	2782	Cousens, J. E.	2 Aug 58	1 Nov 58	
PS	2809	Westcott, R.	6 Aug 58	5 Feb 59	
PS	2810	Pierre, P. A.	6 Aug 58	5 Feb 59	
.PS	2950	Gowland, R. H.	15 Aug 58	14 Nov 58	
WPS	2416	Rice, J.	26 May 57	25 May 58	

SWANSEA BOROUGH

| PS | 2461 | Thomas, J. G. | 3 Oct 57 | 2 Jul 59 | *Special Branch* |
| PS | 2824 | Welch, B. | 6 Aug 58 | 5 Nov 58 | |

TYNEMOUTH BOROUGH

PS	2888	Broad, B. C.	8 Aug 58	16 Feb 60
PS	2889	Hudspith, A.	8 Aug 58	16 Feb 60
PS	2890	Broad, J. S.	8 Aug 58	8 Feb 58

WALLASEY BOROUGH

| PS | 2840 | Kehoe, J. M. | 6 Aug 58 | 5 Feb 59 |

WALSALL BOROUGH

| PS | 2883 | Slater, C. W. | 8 Aug 58 | 8 Feb 59 |

WARRINGTON BOROUGH

| PS | 2954 | Dobbin, E. | 15 Aug 58 | 15 Nov 58 |

PS	2955	Smith, D. T.	15 Aug 58	15 Nov 58	
PS	2956	Crookes, J.	15 Aug 58	15 Nov 58	
PS	2957	Tomlinson, F. G.	15 Aug 58	15 Nov 58	
PS	2958	Jones, F.	15 Aug 58	15 Nov 58	

WARWICKSHIRE COUNTY

SP	256	McKnight, J. P.	25 Aug 56	17 Feb 60	*Awarded the CPM*
Insp	446	Walker, W. J.	25 Aug 56	27 May 58	
ASP	324	Forsythe, G.	26 Sep 56	25 Jun 58	*Awarded the MBE*
ChCon	243	White, G.	9 Jul 56	27 Feb 58	*Awarded the CMG*
Insp	531	Boswell, H. W.	15 Oct 57	16Aug 60	
PS	538	Barrett, T. J.	25 Aug 58	16 Feb 60	
PS	2932	Alsop, E. J.	8 Aug 58	15 Feb 60	
PS	2933	Williams, J. C.	8 Aug 58	9 Feb 59	
WPS	2413	Hildick, G. E.	26 May 57	25 May 58	

WIGAN BOROUGH

| PS | 2969 | Clinch, F. J. V. | 15 Aug 58 | 14 Feb 59 | |

WILTSHIRE COUNTY

| PS | 2260 | Green, A. | 28 Feb 58 | 15 Feb 60 | |

WOLVERHAMPTON BOROUGH

| PS | 2471 | Greaney, R. | 12 Oct 57 | 18 May 59 | |
| PS | 2485 | Bradley, E. A. | 15 Oct 57 | 14 Jul 59 | *Special Branch* |

WORCESTER CITY

| PS | 2531 | Vale, L. R. | 1 Nov 57 | 31 Jul 59 | *CID* |
| PS | 2330 | Cropper, L. W. | 22 Jul 58 | 16 Feb 60 | |

WORCESTERSHIRE COUNTY

PS	2169	Coombe, J.	28 Aug 56	27 May 58	
PS	2168	Fraser, L. J. E.	28 Aug 56	6 Jun 58	
PS	2142	Nash, D. W.	28 Aug 56	16 Feb 60	
PS	2165	Webb, W. I. J.	28 Aug 56	27 May 58	
PS	2140	Young, D. P.	28 Aug 56	16 Feb 60	
PS	1943	Benbow, F. G. A.	11 Sep 58	16 Feb 60	
PS	1870	Morgan, G.	11 Sep 58	17 Feb 60	
Insp	548	Stafford, S. P.	11 Sep 58	26 Oct 59	*Special Branch*
Insp	547	Timmis, K. B.	11 Sep 58	16 Feb 60	
PS	2843	Marpole, G. E.	6 Aug 58	5 Feb 59	
PS	2844	Vale, A.	6 Aug 58	5 Feb 59	
PS	2845	Bairstow, C.	6 Aug 58	5 Nov 58	
WPS	2417	Fisher, R. J.	26 May 57	30 Apr 59	

YORK CITY

PS	2090	Sanderson, H. A.	4 Mar 58	3 Dec 59	
PS	2704	Hollinsworth, J.	20 Jun 58	16 Feb 60	
PS	2705	Parker, H. W.	20 Jun 58	16 Feb 60	
PS	2963	Rhodes, R.	15 Aug 58	15 Nov 58	
WPS	2418	Hutchinson, L. J.	26 May 57	25 May 58	

NORTH RIDING OF YORKSHIRE COUNTY

PS	2264	Roberts, T. E.	26 Sep 56	16 Feb 60	
PS	2265	Deighton, K. M.	26 Sep 56	25 Jun 58	
PS	2266	Smith, P. J.	26 Sep 56	25 Jun 58	
PS	2267	Kilvington, R.	26 Sep 56	25 Jun 58	
PS	2375	Gill, A. J.	25 Apr 57	24 Jan 59	
Insp	530	Wright, J. F.	16 Oct 57	15 Jul 59	
PS	2719	Barry, A.	15 Jul 58	16 Feb 60	
PS	2862	Tulloch, D.	6 Aug 58	6 Nov 58	
PS	2863	Matthews, R.	6 Aug 58	6 Nov 58	
PS	**2864**	**Green, R. H.**	**6 Aug 58**	**4 Feb 59**	

WEST RIDING OF YORKSHIRE COUNTY

Insp	565	French, R. B. N.	7 Jan 56	16 Feb 60	
PS	1738	Critchley, W. E.	7 Jan 56	8 Jun 57	*Died in accident*
PS	1740	Hartshorn, W. M.	7 Jan 56	25 Jul 56	
Insp	482	Dibb, F.	7 Jan 56	20 Oct 59	
PS	1744	Anderson, J.	7 Jan 56	16 Oct 57	*Special Branch*
PS	1745	Lenughan, P. S.	7 Jan 56	25 Sep 59	*CID*
Insp	174	Hailstones, C. H.	7 Jan 56	16 Feb 60	
Insp	173	Turton, W. F.	7 Jan 56	16 Oct 57	
PS	1739	Tully, M. J.	7 Jan 56	12 Mar 56	
PS	2726	Hancock, F.	7 Jan 56	28 Oct 58	*Two tours*
PS	1741	Evans, J. G.	7 Jan 56	4 Oct 59	*CID*
Insp	175	Chester, A. E.	14 Jan 56	23 Oct 57	*CID*
ASP	177	Lawton, G.	14 Jan 56	23 Oct 57	
Insp	525	Egan, V. F.	14 Jan 56	1 Oct 59	*Special Branch*
PS	1747	Re-Foy, P. N. F.	14 Jan 56	23 Oct 57	*CID*
SP	176	Ward, H.	14 Jan 56	16 Feb 60	
Insp	21-	Asquith, T.	11 Apr 56	10 Jan 58	
ACC	252	Stansfield, W.	6 Aug 56	1 Oct 59	*Awarded the CPM*
Insp	526	Butler, T.	25 Apr 57	24 Jan 59	
PS	2328	Kirby, B. S.	15 Oct 56	14 Jul 58	
PS	2335	Ellis, I.	15 Oct 56	14 Jul 58	
PS	2388	Broadley, J. R.	15 Oct 56	13 Jul 58	
PS	2268	Oliver, K.	26 Sep 56	25 Jun 58	
PS	2269	Moorby, D.	26 Sep 56	25 Jun 58	
Insp	554	Harrop, F.	15 Oct 57	14 Jul 59	

PS	2632	Scales, R. M.	28 May 58	16 Feb 60	*CID*
PS	2651	Howland, C. G.	28 May 58	16 Feb 60	
PS	2712	Murphie, J. K.	26 Jun 58	16 Feb 60	
PS	2713	Butterfield, R. M.	26 Jun 58	20 Oct 58	
Insp	536	Mahoney, E. J.	15 Aug 58	14 Feb 60	*CID*
Insp	537	Scott, H.	15 Aug 58	17 Feb 60	*CID*
PS	2871	Petfield, F. J.	6 Aug 58	5 Nov 58	
PS	2872	Dyson, G.	6 Aug 58	16 Feb 60	
PS	2873	Cust, J. E.	6 Aug 58	5 Nov 58	
PS	2874	Fletcher, J.	6 Aug 58	5 Nov 58	
PS	2875	Gothorp, D.	6 Aug 58	5 Nov 58	*CID*
PS	2876	Smith, B. M.	6 Aug 58	5 Nov 58	
PS	2891	Champion, B.	8 Aug 58	8 Feb 59	
PS	2892	Thorpe, G. T.	8 Aug 58	8 Feb 59	
PS	2893	Holdsworth, W.	8 Aug 58	7 Nov 58	
PS	2894	Bailey, W. A.	8 Aug 58	7 Nov 58	
PS	2895	Smith, D. W.	8 Aug 58	16 Feb 60	
PS	2896	Lumb, E. H.	8 Aug 58	7 Nov 58	
PS	2897	Stott, W. G.	8 Aug 58	8 Feb 59	
PS	2898	Lavrie, J.	8 Aug 58	8 Nov 59	
PS	2899	Rhodes, C.	8 Aug 58	8 Feb 59	*CID*
WPS	2612	Chisholm, J.	26 May 58	30 Apr 59	
WPS	2611	Hakins, J.	26 May 58	30 Apr 59	
WPS	2414	Bullock, E. M.	26 May 57	1 Jun 58	
WPS	2415	Dillon, R.	26 May 57	25 May 58	

PS = Police Sergeant
WPS = Woman Police Sergeant
Insp = Inspector
WInsp = Woman Inspector
Supt = Superintendent
WSupt= Woman Superintendent
AsstSupt = Assistant Superintendent
A/ASupt = Acting Assistant Superintendent
ACC = Assistant Chief Constable
ChCon = Chief Constable
CID = Member of Criminal Investigation Department
GM= The George Medal
QPM= The Queen's Police Medal
CPM=The Colonial Police Medal
QCBC=The Queen's Commendation for Brave Conduct
CMG=Companion of the Order of Saint Michael and Saint George
OBE=Officer of the Order of the British Empire
MBE=Member of the Order of the British Empire
BEM= The British Empire Medal (The Medal of the Order of the British Empire)
MDS= Mention for Distinguished Service

In total, 895 police officers served with the UKU, (only counting as one, those officers who did two tours of duty). Of these, 85 (9.5%), were women police officers. The Metropolitan Police was the greatest total supplier, with 146 (16.3%) officers; followed by Lancashire with 53 (5.9%); the West Riding of Yorkshire with 43 (4.8%) officers; and Durham County with 41 (4.5%).

To qualify for the General Service Medal with the 'Cyprus' clasp, a period of service of four months was needed, so it can be inferred that from the service dates above, any officer with four or months service, would qualify for the medal.

APPENDIX 2

HONOURS AND AWARDS OF THE UKU

THE GEORGE MEDAL

Maurice Eden
(Metropolitan Police)
Police Sergeant
London Gazette 18 December 1956, p7146

THE QUEEN'S POLICE MEDAL FOR GALLANTRY
(Posthumous)

Leonard Alfred Demmon
(Metropolitan Police)
Police Sergeant
London Gazette 18 December 1956, p7165

Both awarded for 'The Battle of Nicosia Hospital' see page 38

COLONIAL POLICE MEDAL FOR GALLANTRY

Alan Sewart
(Lancashire County Constabulary)
Police Sergeant
London Gazette 20 August 1957, p4927

No citation is given in the *London Gazette*, so the only information is from a report which appeared in the *Cyprus Mail* on Wednesday 21 August 1957.

Sergeant Sewart (since promoted to Detective Inspector) together with British soldiers, and accompanied by Sergeant 938 Talat Demeriel, a Turkish Cypriot officer of the Cyprus Police, were searching an (unnamed) mountain village. As they were refused entry to a house, Sewart and Demeriel kicked open the door, to be confronted by five men, some of whom were armed.

After a fierce fight, during which miraculously neither officer sustained any gunshot wounds, all five terrorists, and their weapons, were captured by Sewart and Demeriel. Later, more arms and ammunition were captured as a result of information received from this incident.

Alan Sewart was a 29 year old single man, and had been in the Lancashire County Constabulary for 8 years, having been stationed at Bolton. Sergeant Demeriel, a 35 year old officer with 12 years experience and who came from Limassol, also received the Colonial Police Medal for Gallantry.

QUEEN'S COMMENDATION FOR BRAVE CONDUCT

Frederick Adlington Baddeley
(Essex County Constabulary)
Police Sergeant
London Gazette 21 April 1959, p2619
For services when a police car was ambushed by terrorists.

COMPANION OF THE ORDER OF SAINT MICHAEL AND SAINT GEORGE

Geoffrey Charles White
(Warwickshire County Constabulary)
Chief Constable
London Gazette 1 January 1958, p4

OFFICER OF THE ORDER OF THE BRITISH EMPIRE

Thomas Lockley
(Staffordshire County Constabulary)
Acting Assistant Chief Constable (Crime)
London Gazette 1 January 1958, p24

MEMBER OF THE ORDER OF THE BRITISH EMPIRE

George Forsyth
(Warwickshire County Constabulary)
Assistant Superintendent
London Gazette 12 June 1958, p3536

THE BRITISH EMPIRE MEDAL
(THE MEDAL OF THE ORDER OF THE BRITISH EMPIRE)

Sydney Herbert Dabell Brister
(Metropolitan Police)
Detective Inspector
London Gazette 1 January 1960, p32

Neville John Fahy
(Lancashire County Constabulary)
Inspector
London Gazette 1 January 1960, p32

Jeffrey Leach
(Lancashire County Constabulary)
Detective Sergeant
London Gazette 1 January 1958, p3

Joseph Mounsey
(Lancashire County Constabulary)
Detective Sergeant
London Gazette 1 January 1958, p3

John Alan Rollo
(Metropolitan Police)
Inspector
London Gazette 1 January 1960, p32

Gordon Alfred Willard
(Metropolitan Police)
Detective Sergeant
London Gazette 1 January 1958, p3

QUEEN'S POLICE MEDAL
FOR DISTINGUISHED SERVICE

John Edward Stevenson Browne
(Nottinghamshire County Constabulary)
Chief Constable
London Gazette 1 January 1960, p34

Ronald Edward Rowbottom
(Southport Borough Police)
Assistant Chief Constable
London Gazette 1 January 1958, p35
(*also MBE*)

John Robert Webster
(Leicestershire and Rutland Constabulary)
Assistant Chief Constable
London Gazette 12 June 1958, p3546

COLONIAL POLICE MEDAL
FOR MERITORIOUS SERVICE

Winifred Theodora Barker
(Metropolitan Police)
Superintendent
London Gazette 1 January 1959, p34

Robert Stanley Bearne
(Metropolitan Police)
Detective Inspector
London Gazette 1 January 1958, p36

Arthur Burns
(Derby Borough Police)
Assistant Chief Constable
London Gazette 12 June 1958, p3547

James Kenneth England
(Durham County Constabulary
Assistant Superintendent
London Gazette 1 January 1958, p36

Charles Hugh Fraser
(Kent County Constabulary)
Detective Sergeant
London Gazette 13 June 1957, p3405

John James Tawse Grieg
(Angus County Constabulary)
Inspector
London Gazette 12 June 1958, p3547

James Michael Herlihy
(Metropolitan Police)
Superintendent
London Gazette 1 January 1960, p33

John Edward Jackson
(Northumberland County Constabulary)
Sergeant
London Gazette 1 January 1958, p36

Graham Alexander Michael
(Leicestershire and Rutland Constabulary)
Superintendent
London Gazette 1 January 1959, p35

John Patrick McKnight
(Warwickshire County Constabulary)
Superintendent
London Gazette 1 January 1960, p33

Edward Pinhey
(Metropolitan Police)
Assistant Superintendent
London Gazette 1 January 1960, p33

Proven James Sharpe
(Plymouth City Police)
Detective Inspector
London Gazette 13 June 1959, p3730

Walter Stansfield
(West Riding of Yorkshire County Constabulary)
Assistant Chief Constable
London Gazette 13 June 1959, p3730

Arthur James Taylor
(Renfrew and Bute County Constabulary)
Inspector
London Gazette 1 January 1958, p29

Albert Harry White
(Kent County Constabulary)
Superintendent
London Gazette 12 June 1958, p3548

Ronald Willey
(Northamptonshire County Constabulary)
Superintendent
London Gazette 1 January 1959, p35

Harold Wright
(Staffordshire County Constabulary)
Assistant Superintendent
London Gazette 13 June 1957, p3406

MENTIONS FOR DISTINGUISHED SERVICE

On 28 November 1958, p7267, the *London Gazette* published a 'Police List of Mentions for Distinguished Service'. This was, perhaps, the police equivalent of a Mention in Despatches. Two members of the UKU were included, but only initials were used, no first names were given.

E Hollin
(West Sussex County Constabulary)
Sergeant

W L Jones
(Staffordshire County Constabulary)
Inspector

APPENDIX 3

HONOURS AND AWARDS OF
THE CYPRUS POLICE
AND
THE BRITISH COLONIAL POLICE

Although this book is primarily concerned with the UKU, nevertheless, the following is a list of the rest of the awards won by the police forces of Cyprus during the EOKA disturbances.

QUEEN'S POLICE MEDAL FOR GALLANTRY
(Posthumous)

Hussain Nihat Vassif
Police Constable, Cyprus Police
London Gazette 6 November 1956, p6269
For the attempted arrest of an armed gunman during the 1956 Saint George's Day Riots at the Ardath Tobacco Factory, Nicosia. His murderer was chased and caught by Mrs Emine Nevsat, who was awarded the British Empire Medal for Gallantry in the *London Gazette* 9 October 1956, p5683 (see page 30)

COLONIAL POLICE MEDAL FOR GALLANTRY

Demetrius Christou Tsavellas
Police Constable 875, Cyprus Police
London Gazette 26 July 1955, p4308

Hussein Ahmet
Police Constable 737, Cyprus Police
London Gazette 2 March 1956, p1296

Talat Demeriel
Police Sergeant 938, Cyprus Police
London Gazette 20 August 1957, p4927

See the entry for Police Sergeant Alan Sewart of the UKU, who was also awarded the CPM for Gallantry for the same incident.

Timour Mehmet
Police Constable 1362, Cyprus Police
London Gazette 20 August 1957, p4927
Cyprus Mail 21 August 1957

For the capture of armed terrorists at Zoopiyi following a gun fight where one terrorist was killed and two others wounded.

PC Mehmet was later seconded to the Staffordshire County Constabulary for six months, in an exchange scheme.

Houssein Ali Ziya
Police Constable, Cyprus Police
London Gazette 24 January 1958, p534
Cyprus Mail 29 January 1958

On 21 November 1957 PC Ziya was on prison escort duty, when the convoy was ambushed by three terrorists in a village in the Limassol area. Despite being handcuffed to a prisoner, PC Ziya, who was armed with a machine gun, drove off the attackers.

QUEEN'S COMMENDATION FOR BRAVE CONDUCT

Halil Fikret Ahmet
Special Sergeant, Cyprus Special Constabulary
London Gazette 15 July 1958, p4431
For services when an incendiary bomb set fire to boats in
which high explosive bombs had been placed.

Moustafa Ali
Police Constable, Cyprus Police
London Gazette 8 October 1957, p5820
For services when arresting a terrorist about to throw a bomb.

Ozir Hassan Raif
Special Constable, Cyprus Special Constabulary
London Gazette 7 May 1957, p2726
For seizing a grenade which was liable to explode and
throwing it out of lethal range of his comrades.

Mehmet Reshat
Police Sergeant, Cyprus Police
London Gazette 7 May 1957, p2726
For services when attempting to arrest an armed man.

Daniel Socratous
Sub-Inspector, Cyprus Police Fire Brigade
London Gazette 2 December 1958, p7362
For rescuing a mother and child from a burning building.
(Also awarded the CPM, June 1957)

COMMANDER
OF THE ORDER OF THE BRITISH EMPIRE

John Vincent Prendergast
Head of Special Branch, and Chief of Intelligence
London Gazette 1 January 1960, p24
*(A Gazetted British Colonial Police officer, John Prendergast
had been awarded the George Medal whilst in Kenya in May
1955 :* London Gazette *27 September 1955, p5416.
Also awarded the CPM, June 1955)*

OFFICER OF THE ORDER OF THE BRITISH EMPIRE

Frederick Barnaby Carter
Assistant Commissioner
London Gazette 31 May 1956, p3124

Ronald George Locke
Deputy Chief Constable
London Gazette 1 January 1958, p25

Leonard William Whymark
Assistant Chief Constable
London Gazette 12 June 1958, p3536

MEMBER OF THE ORDER OF THE BRITISH EMPIRE

Jack Barlow
Superintendent
London Gazette 1 January 1958, p25

Frederick William Bird
Chief Superintendent
London Gazette 13 June 1957, p3393

Henry John Burge
Superintendent
London Gazette 1 January 1958, p25

Austin Fergus Burke
Superintendent
London Gazette 1 January 1957, p27

Luke Hannon
Superintendent
London Gazette 1 January 1960, p25
(Also CPM, June 1957)

George Meikle
Assistant Chief Constable
London Gazette 1 January 1960, p25

Ahmet Niazi
Assistant Superintendent, Cyprus Police
London Gazette 1 January 1957, p27

Mehmet Refik
Superintendent, Cyprus Police
London Gazette 1 January 1958, p25

Anthony Peter Rice
Assistant Chief Constable
London Gazette 1 January 1960, p25

Richard Otford Russell
Chief Superintendent
London Gazette 1 January 1958, p25

Charles Hugh Johnstone Scott
Chief Superintendent
London Gazette 13 June 1957, p3393

Vehid Salih Soubhi
Local Commandant, Cyprus Special Constabulary
London Gazette 13 June 1957, p3393

Archibald Francis Thompson
Chief Superintendent
London Gazette 1 January 1960, p25
(Also CPM, June 1957)

John Zachariades
Local Commandant, Cyprus Special Constabulary
London Gazette 13 June 1957, p3393

THE BRITISH EMPIRE MEDAL
(THE MEDAL OF THE ORDER OF THE BRITISH EMPIRE)

William Frederick Owers
Special Constable, Cyprus Emergency Special Constabulary
London Gazette 1 January 1957, p34

Enis Rushen Salih
Police Sergeant, Cyprus Police
London Gazette 1 January 1960, p32

QUEEN'S POLICE MEDAL
FOR DISTINGUISHED SERVICE

James Hector McDonald Williams
Superintendent
London Gazette 1 January 1959 p34

QUEEN'S POLICE AND FIRE SERVICES MEDAL

Socrates Charalambous
Sub Inspector, Cyprus Police Fire Brigade
London Gazette 13 June 1957, p3404

COLONIAL POLICE MEDAL
FOR MERITORIOUS SERVICE

Included in the *London Gazette*, 1 January 1955, p38
Paschalis Savvides
Chief Inspector, Cyprus Police

Osman Zekki
Chief Inspector, Cyprus Police

Included in the *London Gazette* 9 June 1955, p3295
John Vincent Prendergast
Senior Superintendent

Panos Prodromitis
Chief Inspector, Cyprus Police

Included in the *London Gazette* 2 January 1956, p37
Costas Constantinides
Sergeant Major, Cyprus Police

Costas Petrou Georghiades
Inspector, Cyprus Police

Mehmet Kiamil
Local Commandant, Cyprus Special Constabulary

Michael Pentelides
Inspector, Cyprus Police

Abdullah Ali Riza
Police Sergeant, Cyprus Police
(PS Riza was murdered on 11th January 1956)

Included in the *London Gazette* 31 May 1956, p3137
Ali Faik
Police Sergeant, Cyprus Police

Apostolos Papaconstantinou
Chief Inspector, Cyprus Police

Included in the *London Gazette* 1 January 1957, p38
Mustafa Ahmed
Police Sergeant, Cyprus Police

Fylactis Aristokleous
Sub-Inspector, Cyprus Police

Demetrios Michael
Detective Inspector, Cyprus Police

Kiazin Nami
Assistant Superintendent, Cyprus Police

Kemal Osman
Police Sergeant, Cyprus Police

Included in the *London Gazette* 13 June 1957, p3405
Luke Hannon
Superintendent

Hassan Houloussi
Police Sergeant, Cyprus Police

Houssein Mehmed
Inspector, Cyprus Police

Nicolas Michael Mezos
Superintendent, Cyprus Police

Ali Radji
Assistant Superintendent, Cyprus Police

Daniel Socratous
Police Sergeant, Cyprus Police Fire Brigade
(also awarded QCBC, December 1958)

Archibald Francis Thompson
Superintendent
(also awarded MBE, January 1960)

Norman Peter Widdowson
Assistant Superintendent

Included in the *London Gazette* 1 January 1958, p36
John Dudley Brawn
Superintendent

Robert Arthur Clarke
Superintendent
(already holding the MBE)

Yashir Halil Hassan
Police Sergeant, Cyprus Police

William Edward Henry Holdsworth
Assistant Superintendent

Michael Elia Petridis
Police Sergeant, Cyprus Police

Mehmet Suleiman
Police Sergeant, Cyprus Police

Brian John Dereck Sullivan
Assistant Superintendent

Theodoros Constantinou Theocharides
Inspector, Cyprus Police

Included in the *London Gazette* 12 June 1958, p3548
Robert Audley Patrick Herbert Dutton
Acting Assistant Chief Constable
(Already holding the DFC)

Kemal Hifzi
Sub-Inspector, Cyprus Police

Edward Norman Pierce
Superintendent

Nicolas Savvides
Sub-Inspector, Cyprus Police

Included in the *London Gazette* 1 January 1959, p35
Demosthenes Constantinou Rigas
Assistant Superintendent, Cyprus Police

Arthur Herbert Turner
Chief Inspector

Pangalos Victor Zachariades
Assistant Fire Officer, Cyprus Police Fire Brigade

Included in the *London Gazette* 13 June 1959, p3730
Haralambos Potsalides
Chief Inspector, Cyprus Police

Included in the *London Gazette* 1 January 1960, p33
Sydney James Gander
Superintendent

Salih Hassan
Superintendent, Cyprus Police

Demetrios Issais
Assistant Superintendent, Cyprus Police

MENTIONS FOR DISTINGUISHED SERVICE

On page 7267 of the *London Gazette* of 28 November 1958, was published a list of 'Mentions for Distinguished Service', which perhaps is equivalent to a Mention in Despatches. Included in the list are the following :

Houssein Ahmed Detective Sergeant, Cyprus Police
Zekiayi Ali Lance Corporal, Cyprus Auxiliary Police
Mehmet Dilaver Lance Corporal, Cyprus Auxiliary Police
Behitch Dilaver Police Sergeant, Cyprus Police
Boulent Djemel Police Constable, Cyprus Police
Mustafa Halil Police Constable, Cyprus Police
Mehmet Hassan Detective Sergeant, Cyprus Police
Savvas Ioannou Police Sergeant, Cyprus Police
Errol Ismail Police Constable, Cyprus Police
Mustafa Izzet Police Constable, Cyprus Police
Salih Kadir Sergeant, Cyprus Auxiliary Police
Ahmet Mehmet Police Constable, Cyprus Police
Houssein Mehmed Police Constable, Cyprus Police
Rashid Mehmed Police Constable, Cyprus Police
Bayram Mouharrem Police Constable, Cyprus Auxiliary Police
Ismail Mustafa Inspector, Cyprus Police
George Neoclesus Police Constable, Cyprus Police
Agapios Papaconstantinou Sub-Inspector, Cyprus Police
Enis Saleh Police Sergeant, Cyprus Police
Izzet Shakir Police Constable, Cyprus Police
Hamit Zoubeir Police Constable, Cyprus Police

Also included are: (sic – only initials given)
E Sweet Major, Detention Camp Department
FG Howard-Willis Major, Detention Camp Department
WF Hayman Detention Camp Department

131

APPENDIX 4

The day-to-day duties of the Officers of the UKU, are best illustrated by a selection of duties taken from the Pocket Book of PS 2869 R. Watson, UKU, whose home force was the Northamptonshire County Constabulary.

Wednesday 17 September 1958

Tour 8am x 12 md: 2pm x 6pm

Mobile reserve patrols with PS 2870 *(PS Peter Holyoak, also of the Northamptonshire County Constabulary)*

4.30pm Road check on Nicosia to Kakopetria road outside Grenadier Guards Camp. Bus travelling to Kakopetria searched. Greek leaflet found by PC2025 *(A Constable of the Cyprus Police, and obviously Turkish Cypriot).* Ascertained owned by A------ K------ - (18) b 29/11/39, I/C No. 10412 of Kakopetria Village. Searched his suitcase and found a number of same type of leaflets. Unable to translate. Arrested him and took him to S/B Central Police Station for further enquiry. N/A of bus driver: I------ K------- (26) of Kakopetria. I/C No. 10580. D/L No. 29442.

Thursday 18th September 1958

Tour 8am x 12md: 2pm x 8pm

Duty with Mobile Reserve in company with PS 2870. Checks and searches made Lamocu (?) road, Agios Demetrios and Nicosia. Visited scenes of shootings of R.A.F. Servicemen (2 Turks) and Santa Rosa Street. 1 American. Areas patrolled.

Friday 19 September 1958

Tour 8am x 12md: 2pm x 6pm

Mobile patrols in company with PS 2870 with Mobile Reserve. Checks and searches made

3.0pm Clearchos Street, Nicosia. Check made at Coffee House at 2B of above street. Following Greeks produced Identity Cards which showed they were born between 1/1/33 and 1/1/43 (in other words, between the ages of 15 1/2 and 25 1/2, which made them subject to

132

the British imposed House Curfew) (1)K-----C----------- b. 10/7/36 Blacksmith of 1 Clearchos Street, I/C No. 245578. (2) A------ T----, Fitter of 1 Clearchos Street, I/C No. 182804B. 12/11/36. (3) G------- T------- B. 22/1/35 I/C No. 191825 Pipe and Tube Fitter of Neonkharian (?) Village. house Curfew imposed on Greek males 15 1/2 - 25 1/2. Above not in possession of valid Curfew Passes. Arrested and taken to Central Police Station

3.15pm where seen by PS 97 Peter. Offences pointed out to them by him in Greek. Explanations: C said "It is near our houses". T said "We came out of our house to get air". T said "We came out of our house to get air". PS97 told them they would be reported.

4.00pm Continued patrol in Nicosia Town

Sunday 28 September 1958

Tour 2pm x 10pm

Detailed [foot patrol in the] area Paphos Gate and 'Mason Dixon Line'

(The Paphos Gate is one of the gates through the medieval circular walls which still surround the old city of Nicosia; the Mason Dixon Line was the nickname for the dividing line between the Greek and Turkish quarters of the city) with PS 2870 *(PS P. Holyoak, Northamptonshire County Constabulary)*, PS2996 *(PS R. Stewart, Renfrew and Bute Constabulary)* and PC 2116 *(a Turkish Cypriot policeman of the Cyprus Police)*

7.30pm Coffee

8.15pm Resumed patrol

10pm Duty completed

Saturday 4 October 1958

Tour 6am x 2pm

Detailed guard duty in Turkish ward of Nicosia General Hospital.

6.15pm Nicosia General Hospital

9am Refreshments

9.45 resumed guard duty at Nicosia General Hospital

2pm Completed duty

Monday 5 January 1959
Tour 2pm x 10pm
Detailed Mobile Section 1
2pm Commenced patrol
5.40pm Report of incident 104 Hermes Street, possible shooting. Visited immediately. Ascertained A---------- T-------- (40) Shopkeeper had been struck on head by pistol [shot] and conveyed to Nicosia General Hospital. One .38 magazine (full) found at scene. Witness I------- A-----, 13 Arsinos Street, Strovolos. Conveyed to Nicosia Central Police Station
7.15pm Refreshment
8pm Resumed patrol
10pm Off duty

APPENDIX 5

To be required to carry a gun at all times must have seemed unnatural to the normally unarmed British police officer. But although a good proportion of the UKU police officers had been in the armed forces and had had some acquaintance with firearms, nevertheless, there were some that had not. They were unused to coping with the realisation that carrying a weapon, made them an automatic target for terrorist gunmen, more so off duty than on, and therefore their vigilance and observation of the world about them, must be heightened accordingly.

To emphasise the extra vigilance required, two types of printed cards were issued to every member of the UKU, reminding them that EOKA considered them to be legitimate targets. And as such, these cards gave advice on the best way to minimize, or deal with, any danger.

Both these cards are reproduced verbatim:

"RESTRICTED

Men have been killed and wounded lately through their own carelessness. Every Policeman and Government Official is an E.O.K.A. target.

The following instructions are a guide to help you in your normal day to day routine duties. they do not cover all aspects of precautions that can be taken but if remembered will stand you in good stead and may well deter an assailant.

Always remember that a potential assailant can study you without your knowing it and always has that advantage. You must be on the watch at all times. remember above all, that HABIT may destroy.

1. A. Always carry a loaded revolver.

   B. DON'T, unless quite unavoidable, go out alone unarmed.

2. A. If it is necessary to shoot in self protection or in protection of another, stand steady, shoot quickly and accurately.

   B. DON'T attempt to shoot at an assailant whilst you are running, you will not hit him.

3. A. If you have a driver bodyguard, use him at all times, on or off duty.

   B. DON'T just take a chance and not take your bodyguard with you.

4. A. Keep changing your routes and times to and from the places you are visiting.

   B. DON'T use the same route every day at the same time.

5. A. Keep your eyes open for persons lurking in the vicinity of your house, office, or Police Station when you enter or leave.

   B. DON'T walk out of your house, office or Police Station dreaming and not knowing what goes on about you.

6. A. be constantly alert whenever youths on bicycles are in your vicinity.

   B. DON'T ignore youths on bicycles.

7. A. When driving your car, place your revolver under your right thigh, so as to be in easy reach of your hand.

B. DON'T have your pistol where you cannot get at it whilst driving your car yourself.

8. A. Have your revolver in your hand whilst travelling as a passenger in a vehicle.

B. DON'T have your pistol where you cannot get at it whilst riding as a passenger in a vehicle.

9. A. Avoid as much as possible routes that may lead you into traffic jams.

B. DON'T use routes that are prone to traffic jams.

10. A. Keep moving. Far better to back out and change direction than be stuck in some narrow street.

B. DON'T stop your vehicle and just sit waiting to move, and not keep an eye on what goes on about you.

11. A. When in your quarters check your telephone from time to time to ascertain that it is in working order.

B. DON'T just ignore your telephone and expect it to work when you want it to.

12. A. Always let a male member of your household answer all calls at night.

B. DON'T let a female member of your household answer it at night. The other side may think that no males are in the house and take advantage of it.

13. A. Always answer your door armed and be on the alert.

B. DON'T just take a chance and answer the door unarmed, and think that the other side would dare not to come to your door.

14. A. Always put out your hall light and put on the outside light when answering your door at night.

B. DON'T silhouette yourself at night in a lighted doorway.

136

15. A. Use alternative exits from your home if you have them. Open the door quietly and slip out quietly. At night accustom your eyes to the darkness before slipping out.

B. DON'T use the same exit all the time and go out of light into darkness immediately. You will not be able to see.

16. A. When ion or off duty outside your house or office, take precautions against surprise attacks from the rear (eg Make sure that your back is to the wall or, if that is not possible, arrange for another officer to cover you from the rear.

B. DON'T walk about in a dream.

17. A. If on foot avoid the centre of the road, keep on the side of the road and pay particular attention to corners of buildings, side streets, shops and doorways, bearing in mind that an assailant can always attack from the roof of a house.

B. DON'T think that YOU are immune from attack.

18. A. When two or more officers are together, never walk side by side or close together, walk a tactical bound of 10-15 yards behind each other and on alternative sides of the road.

B. DON'T think that because you are unimportant you are safe."

The second card deals with the harrowing question, 'when should I open fire?'

"Restricted
INSTRUCTIONS TO INDIVIDUALS FOR OPENING FIRE IN CYPRUS ISSUED BY CHIEF OF STAFF TO H.E. THE GOVERNOR

1. INDIVIDUAL RESPONSIBILITY
Before you use force it is always your duty to assess the situation confronting you and to decide what degree of force is necessary.

If having done this carefully and honestly, you decide that there is no alternative but to open fire, and then do so, you will be doing your duty and acting lawfully whatever the consequences.

2. WHEN YOU SHOULD FIRE

It is your duty to shoot if that is the only way:

(a) To defend yourself, your comrades, families, Police and all peaceable inhabitants against serious attack.

(b) To protect against serious damage [to] all Government property, eg buildings, installations, vehicles and equipment.

(c) To disperse a riotous mob that you honestly believe will cause serious injury to life and property if not forcibly prevented.

(d) To arrest persons committing acts of violence, or whom you honestly believe have done so, or are about to do so, and to prevent their escape.

3. WHEN YOU SHOULD NOT FIRE

(a) If it is obvious that you can achieve your object by other means, do not shoot

(b) If you are a member of a party under the orders of a superior, do not fire until he orders you to do so.

4. HOW TO FIRE

(a) Always fire aimed shots

(b) Aim at the part of the body you are least likely to miss, i.e. in the middle

(c) Never fire warning shots over people's heads.

5 SENTRIES AND PICQUETS

(a) If you or the persons or place you are guarding are attacked with arms or explosives, open fire at once.

(b) If you think you are about to be attacked in any way, challenge loudly, bring your weapon to the aim and call out the guard. If the person challenged halts, get a member of the guard to investigate. If he does not and you really believe that he is about to attack you with arms or explosives shoot him at once; otherwise try to halt him with your bayonet.

6 ESCORTS

(a) If you, your driver, passengers or vehicles are attacked with arms or explosives open fire at once and tell the driver to keep going and get away.

(b) If you are only stoned tell your driver to keep going and get away. Don't fire unless the stoning is so serious that you really believe the vehicle may be stopped altogether and that you, the driver or your passengers, will be seriously injured.

(c) If your vehicle is obstructed by a road block try to remove it. If you are then attacked with arms or explosives, open fire.

(d) Always be on the alert with your weapon at the ready.

7 INDIVIDUAL SELF DEFENCE

(a) If you are attacked with arms or explosives shoot the attackers at once, wherever you are.

(b) Don't join in brawls. Always avoid trouble if you can.

8 REPORTS

You must always report to the nearest Police or Military Post giving details:-

(a) Location
(b) Details
(c) Method of attack
(d) Description of assailants
(e) When applicable, number of rounds fired and results.

BIBLIOGRAPHY

BARKER, Barry, BROWN, Gavin, BURKE, Terry *Police as Peace- Keepers*
UNCIVPOL, Victoria, Australia 1984

COYLE, Dominick J. *Minorities in Revolt*
Associated University Presses 1983

FOLEY, Charles *Legacy of Strife*
Penguin 1964

GEORGIADES, Cleanthis *History of Cyprus*
Demetrakis Christophourou, Engomi, Cyprus 1995

HOME, Gordon *Cyprus then and now*
J. M. Dent 1960

PENTELI, Stavros *The Making of Modern Cyprus*
Interworld Publications 1990

SERAPHIM-LOIZOU, Elenitsa *The Cyprus Liberation Struggle 1955-1959: Through the eyes of a woman E.O.K.A. Area Commander*
Epiphaniou Publications, Cyprus

STILES, Richard G.M.L. *Mayhem in the Med: A Chronicle of the Cyprus Emergency 1955-1960*
Savannah Publications, London 2005

THUBRON, Colin *Journey into Cyprus*
Travel Book Club 1976

VANEZIS, P. N. *Makarios: Pragmatism v. Idealism*
Abelard-Schuman 1974

WHITCOMB, George *Bullet. Rope. Guillotine*
Aintree Publishing 1995

The London Gazette
The Times
The Cyprus Mail
The Cyprus Times

ACKNOWLEDGEMENTS

Firstly, my thanks go to my brother-in-law and sister-in-law, Stan and Maureen Chalker, who initially introduced me to the unforgettable island of Cyprus. Thus, in a way, they started off the process which has resulted in this book. Although I had previously known of the UKU - and indeed had served with two members of it during my own police career - my first visit to Cyprus made such an impression on me, that I was determined to compile the story of the UKU myself, when I found that, not unsurprisingly, no history of it was available. To Stan and Maureen I offer my thanks.

I also offer thanks to the following : Mr Frank Cluer, sometime Secretary of the UKU Old Comrades' Association, who gave me a lot of information and names and addresses, including Mr B. Boswell of Corsham, Wiltshire (for the personnel list and research); Mr R. Tomlin of Gravesend, Kent (for lots of photographs); and Mr N. Halford of Banbury, Oxfordshire (for local newspapers), all members of the UKU, and who freely lent me their own personal memories. Also to my two old comrades, Tom Pell of Thrapston, and Peter Holyoake of Corby. I would also thank the family of Sergeant Hugh Carter, who gave permission to photograph his last resting place, and for his photograph, for which I also thank the Chief Constable of West Mercia Constabulary, as well as for the photograph of the Worcestershire contingent. For the photographs of Sergeants Woodward and Coote, I thank the Chief Constable of Durham Constabulary. For permission to reproduce the Pocket Book of Sergeant Watson, I thank the Chief Constable of Northamptonshire Police.

Thanks are also due to the Dean of Saint Paul's Cathedral in Nicosia, the Very Reverend Steve Collis, for his interest, and for allowing the photographs of the Memorial Candlesticks and Cross. To Major John Casey of the British High Commission in Cyprus, for his thoughts, and for obtaining the permission to photograph the graves in the British Cemetery in Nicosia. To the Reverend A. A. Mustoe, Vicar of All Saints Church, Orpington; the Reverend D. Palmer, of Saint Joseph's Church, Culfeightrin, County Antrim; Mr Michael Henderson, General Manager of the New Southgate Cemetery; and to Mr Roger Parker, Cemeteries Officer, Royal Borough of Kensington and Chelsea, who all gave permission to photograph the graves within their care, I offer thanks.

My visits to the offices of the *Cyprus Mail* in Nicosia were always a joy for me, and I thank the editor and his staff for their courtesy.

The Crown copyright material is reproduced under Click-Use PSI Licence number C2008000521.